Low Cholesterol

Cookbook 2023

1800+ Irresistible Low Cholesterol Recipes to Strengthen Heart Protection and Reduce Kidney Burden in a Vibrant 28-day Meal Plan

Tawana R. Anthony

CONTENTS

Poultry 35

Fish And Seafood 48

Soups, Salads, And Sides 61

Vegetarian Mains 73

Desserts And Treats 86

Appendix A : Measurement Conversions 98

Appendix B : Recipes Index 100

INTRODUCTION

It is with immense pleasure and pride that I present to you "Low Cholesterol Recipes 2023", a labor of love, a guide to healthier living, and a testament to the belief that food should be both delicious and good for you.

I have long held the conviction that health is wealth and that the path to wellness does not have to be a daunting journey of deprivation and denial. Instead, it can be a delightful adventure filled with exploration, experimentation, and, yes, enjoyment of the varied bounties of nature that are beneficial to our bodies.

Heart health is close to my heart, so to speak. The rising incidence of cardiovascular diseases, largely due to unhealthy diets and sedentary lifestyles, had me searching for a way to combat this. As a culinary enthusiast and wellness advocate, I wanted to create a resource that would enable people to change their eating habits, without feeling like they're giving up the joy of food. And thus, "Low Cholesterol Recipes 2023" was born. This book was born from the passion to create tasty, creative meals that can be enjoyed by anyone, even if you're on a low-cholesterol diet. The recipes you'll find in this collection are not just heart-friendly, but they're also packed with vibrant flavors and diverse ingredients that will bring joy back into your kitchen.

The "Low Cholesterol Recipes 2023" is more than just a recipe book - it's a testament to the fact that a diet for health does not have to come at the expense of enjoying what we eat. I've combined the latest nutritional advice with a global array of flavors to provide recipes that will help you maintain your cholesterol levels without sacrificing the pleasure of a good meal. Throughout the pages of this book, you'll find everything from sumptuous breakfasts and hearty main dishes to delicious desserts and snacks - all designed to fit seamlessly into a low-cholesterol diet. Each recipe is accompanied by nutritional information to help you make informed choices and manage your cholesterol levels more effectively.

Enjoy the journey to heart health, one delicious meal at a time.

Cholesterol is a waxy, fat-like substance that is found in all the cells in your body. Your body needs some cholesterol to make hormones, vitamin D, and substances that help you digest foods. It is also an essential component of cell membranes, required for maintaining structural integrity and fluidity. Cholesterol doesn't dissolve in blood. Instead, it's transported through your bloodstream in small packages called lipoprotein, which are made up of fat on the inside and proteins on the outside.

Below are the total fat saturated fat cholesterol content of some ingredients, please note that these values will vary slightly depending on the cooking method and the specific ingredient.

Cholesterol and Fat in Foods (Before Cooking)			
Food	**Total Fat**	**Saturated Fat**	**Cholesterol**
Chicken breast (4 ounces)	4.05 grams	1.15 grams	96.39 mg
Flank steak (4 ounces)	9.37 grams	3.89 grams	46.33 mg
Ground beef (4 ounces; 85 percent lean)	16.80 grams	6.57 grams	76.16 mg
Shrimp (4 ounces)	1.96 grams	0.37 grams	172.27 mg
Salmon (4 ounces)	12.30 grams	2.47 grams	66.87 mg
Ground turkey (4 ounces)	9.42 grams	2.56 grams	90.06 mg
Pork tenderloin (4 ounces)	6.14 grams	2.12 grams	74.84 mg
Olive oil (1 tablespoon)	13.50 grams	1.86 grams	0.0 mg
Almonds (¼ cup)	18.42 grams	1.42 grams	0.0 mg
Egg yolk (large)	4.51 grams	1.62 grams	209.78 mg

Elevated levels of LDL cholesterol — often called "bad cholesterol" — can lead to the development of fatty deposits in your blood vessels, increasing your risk of heart disease and stroke. Some foods are particularly high in saturated and trans fats, which can raise your cholesterol levels. Here are foods that are best to limit or avoid if you're trying to manage your cholesterol:

Trans Fats: Often found in margarines, store-bought pastries, cookies, cakes, and fried foods. Trans fats raise overall cholesterol levels. The FDA has banned the use of partially hydrogenated oils, the major source of artificial trans fats, but some foods may still contain them.

Organ Meats: Organ meats like liver and kidney are high in cholesterol, even though they are also rich in nutrients.

Fried Foods: Fried foods, especially those from fast-food restaurants, are high in trans fats and saturated fats.

Certain Seafoods: Some shellfish and fish, while generally healthier than red meat, can be high in cholesterol. However, they also contain healthy omega-3 fats.

Shellfish and Organ Meats: While these can be good sources of certain nutrients, they're also high in cholesterol.

It's important to remember that dietary cholesterol does not affect everyone the same way, and for many people, foods high in saturated and trans fats are more likely to raise their cholesterol levels than foods high in dietary cholesterol. For heart health, the focus should be on eating a variety of nutrient-rich foods that are high in fiber and low in saturated and trans fats.

What are the benefits of sticking to a cholesterol diet?

Sticking to a low-cholesterol diet or a diet that helps manage cholesterol levels can offer numerous benefits, especially when it comes to heart health. These benefits include:

• **Improved Heart Health**: A low-cholesterol diet can help decrease the amount of low-density lipoprotein (LDL, or "bad") cholesterol and increase high-density lipoprotein (HDL, or "good") cholesterol levels in your body. This can reduce the risk of plaque build-up in your arteries, a significant cause of heart disease and stroke.

• **Improved Digestive Health:** A cholesterol-friendly diet often involves increased fiber intake, which can improve digestive health by preventing constipation and promoting overall gut health.

• **Improved Digestive Health:** Diets high in fiber, often recommended for managing cholesterol, can also help improve digestive health by reducing the risk of constipation, diverticular disease, and hemorrhoids.

• **Preventing Artery Damage:** High cholesterol levels can lead to the buildup of plaque in the arteries, a condition known as atherosclerosis. This can narrow or block the arteries, leading to heart attack or stroke. A cholesterol-conscious diet can help prevent this.

• **Weight Management:** High cholesterol is often associated with being overweight or obese. A diet that includes plenty of fruits, vegetables, lean proteins, and whole grains can also help you manage your weight.

• **Reduced Risk of Stroke**: By helping to lower the level of cholesterol in your blood, a low-cholesterol diet can help reduce the risk of stroke.

• **Increased Lifespan:** With the reduction of heart disease and stroke risks, individuals following a low-cholesterol diet may potentially increase their overall lifespan.

Remember, a low-cholesterol diet doesn't mean you have to give up flavor or satisfaction in your meals. There are countless delicious recipes and food options available that can help manage cholesterol while also meeting your dietary needs and preferences. It's also essential to incorporate regular physical activity alongside dietary changes for the best results.

28 Day Meal Plan

	Breakfast	Lunch	Dinner
Day 1	Italian Baked Omelet 11	Beef-risotto–stuffed Peppers 23	Filet Mignon With Vegetables 28
Day 2	Fruity Oat-nut Trail Bars 11	Fruit-stuffed Pork Tenderloin 23	Chicken Breasts With Salsa 41
Day 3	Egg Foo Young 12	Whole-wheat Spaghetti And Meatballs 24	Tangy Fish And Tofu Soup 62
Day 4	Pumpkin Oatmeal Smoothies 13	Classic Spaghetti And Meatballs 24	Summer Pineapple Fruit Salad 63
Day 5	Green Tea And Raspberry Smoothies 11	Mini Lasagna Cups 25	Broccoli Slaw 63
Day 6	Avocado And Kiwi Green Smoothies 13	Wasabi-roasted Filet Mignon 25	Watermelon, Edamame, And Radish Salad 64
Day 7	Whole-grain Cornbread 14	Pork Chops With Smoky Barbecue Rub 25	Fresh Creamy Fruit Dip 64
Day 8	Carrot-oatmeal Bread 13	Beef With Mushroom Kabobs 26	Apple Coleslaw 65
Day 9	Cashew & Berry Shake 14	Bbq Pork Chops 27	Barbeque Tofu Salad 65
Day 10	Maghrebi Poached Eggs 14	Pork And Fennel Stir Fry 29	Banana To Go 65
Day 11	Chocolate Pancakes 15	Pork Skewers With Cherry Tomatoes 29	Indian Vegetable Soup 66
Day 12	Amaranth And Date Porridge 15	Beef And Broccoli 30	Hearty Bean And Quinoa Stew 67
Day 13	Roasted Garlic Bread 15	Pork Chops With Mustard Sauce 31	Tangy Mint Salad 68
Day 14	Cinnamon-hazelnut Scones 16	Grilled Coffee-rubbed Sirloin Steak 32	Fennel-and-orange Salad 67

	Breakfast	Lunch	Dinner
Day 15	Spicy Salmon Avocado Sandwich 16	Stir-fried Crispy Orange Beef 32	Corn And Tomato Bean Salad 68
Day 16	Whole-grain Oatmeal Bread 17	Pork Scallops With Spinach 33	Balsamic Vinaigrette 68
Day 17	Navajo Chili Bread 17	Canadian-bacon Risotto 34	Caramelized Spiced Carrots 69
Day 18	Cornmeal-cranberry Rolls 18	Pork Cutlets With Fennel And Kale 34	Winter Noodle Soup 69
Day 19	Spinach Artichoke Pizza 18	Grilled Turkey And Veggie Kabobs 36	Black Bean Soup 70
Day 20	Cranberry-orange Bread 19	Tandoori Turkey Pizzas 36	Low-sodium Beef Broth 70
Day 21	Blueberry Breakfast Muffins 19	Chicken Paillards With Mushrooms 37	Stuffed Jalapeño Peppers 71
Day 22	Nutty Quinoa Waffles 20	Moroccan Chicken 37	Scalloped Potatoes With Aromatic Vegetables 71
Day 23	Orange-vanilla Smoothie 20	Balsamic Blueberry Chicken 38	Salmon Pâté 72
Day 24	Protein Cereal 21	Piri Piri Chicken 38	Greek Quesadillas 72
Day 25	Beef Rollups With Pesto 27	Hawaiian Chicken Stir-fry 39	Ratatouille 74
Day 26	Western Omelet 30	Turkey Curry With Fruit 39	Garbanzo Sandwich 74
Day 27	Beef Burrito Skillet 31	Chicken Spicy Thai Style 40	Bean And Veggie Cassoulet 75
Day 28	Meatball Pizza 33	Asian Chicken Stir-fry 41	Spinach-ricotta Omelet 76

Breakfast And Brunch

Italian Baked Omelet

Servings: 2
Cooking Time: 20 Min

Ingredients:
- Cooking spray
- 6 large free-range egg whites
- ¼ cup unsweetened soy milk
- ½ tsp basil, chopped
- Himalayan pink salt
- Ground black pepper
- ¼ cup green beans, chopped
- ¼ cup red bell pepper, chopped
- ½ spring onion, chopped
- 2 tbsp. fat-free cheddar cheese, shredded

Directions:
1. Preheat the oven to 350°F gas mark 4. Grease 2 medium ramekins with cooking spray and set aside.
2. In a medium-sized mixing bowl, add the egg whites, soy milk, and basil, whisk until well blended. Season with salt and pepper, set aside.
3. Divide the green beans, red bell pepper, and spring onion between the 2 ramekins and pour in the egg white mixture. Top each ramekin with 1 tbsp. of cheddar cheese.
4. Bake for 15 to 20 minutes, until the baked omelet has puffed up and lightly browned. Serve hot.

Nutrition Info:
- Info Per Serving: Calories: 126 ; Fat: 4 g ;Saturated fat: 2 g ;Sodium: 164 mg

Green Tea And Raspberry Smoothies

Servings: X
Cooking Time: X

Ingredients:
- 1 green tea bag
- ½ cup boiling water
- 2 cups unsweetened vanilla almond or soy milk
- 2 cups frozen raspberries
- 1 zucchini, cut into chunks
- 2 tablespoons honey
- ½ teaspoon chopped fresh mint

Directions:
1. In a mug, steep the tea bag in the boiling water for 4 to 5 minutes.
2. Remove the bag, squeezing it out into the mug, and place the tea in the refrigerator to cool completely, 45 minutes to 1 hour.
3. In a blender, add the cooled tea, milk, raspberries, zucchini, honey, and mint and blend until very smooth.
4. Pour into glasses and serve immediately.

Nutrition Info:
- Info Per Serving: Calories: 274; Fat: 5 g ;Saturated fat: 1 g ;Sodium: 136 mg

Fruity Oat-nut Trail Bars

Servings: 2
Cooking Time: X

Ingredients:
- 1 cup brown sugar
- ¼ cup canola oil
- 1 egg
- ½ cup orange juice
- ¼ cup oatmeal
- 1/3 cup all-purpose flour
- 1 teaspoon baking powder
- 1 teaspoon baking soda
- 3 egg whites
- ½ cup chopped walnuts
- ½ cup dried cranberries
- ½ cup golden raisins

Directions:
1. Preheat oven to 300ºF. Spray a 9″ × 13″ glass baking dish with nonstick cooking spray containing flour, and set aside.
2. In large bowl, combine brown sugar, canola oil, egg, and orange juice and mix well. Stir in oatmeal, flour, baking powder, and baking soda until moistened.
3. In small bowl, beat egg whites until stiff. Fold into oat mixture along with walnuts, cranberries, and raisins. Spread into prepared pan.
4. Bake for 45 to 55 minutes or until bars are set and golden brown. Let cool for 20 minutes, then cut into bars. Wrap bars individually in plastic wrap to store.

Nutrition Info:
- Info Per Serving: Calories:124.17 ; Fat:4.44 g ;Saturated fat: 0.38 g;Sodium: 81.62 mg

Egg Foo Young

Servings: 2 – 4
Cooking Time: 10 Min

Ingredients:
- Cooking spray
- ½ medium red bell pepper, chopped
- ½ medium green bell pepper, chopped
- ¼ cup red onion, finely chopped
- ¼ cup Roma tomatoes, chopped
- ¼ cup lean ham, chopped
- 2½ cups large egg whites
- ½ tsp basil, chopped
- Fine sea salt
- Ground black pepper

Directions:
1. Spray a medium nonstick frying pan with cooking spray and place it over medium heat.
2. Add the red and green bell peppers, onion, tomato, and ham to the pan and fry for 4 minutes until tender.
3. Add the egg whites into the pan, over the ham mixture, and cook for 1 minute, until just beginning to set. Use a rubber spatula or turner and gently lift the edges of the setting egg whites, while tilting the pan to allow any uncooked egg to run beneath. Continue this process for 3 minutes until all the egg whites are set.
4. Remove the pan from the heat and fold one side of the egg white omelet over the other.
5. Cut the omelet in half and sprinkled with chopped basil and seasoned with fine sea salt and ground black pepper. Serve warm.

Nutrition Info:
- Info Per Serving: Calories: 215 ; Fat: 2g ;Saturated fat: 0g ;Sodium: 469 mg

Pumpkin Oatmeal Smoothies

Servings: X
Cooking Time: X

Ingredients:

- 2 cups unsweetened soy milk
- 1 cup puréed canned pumpkin
- ½ cup rolled oats
- 1 tablespoon hemp hearts
- 1 tablespoon blackstrap molasses
- ¼ teaspoon ground cinnamon
- ⅛ teaspoon ground nutmeg
- ⅛ teaspoon ground ginger

Directions:

1. In a blender, add the soy milk, pumpkin, oats, hemp hearts, molasses, cinnamon, nutmeg, and ginger and purée until smooth.
2. Pour into glasses and serve immediately.

Nutrition Info:

- Info Per Serving: Calories: 322; Fat: 9 g ;Saturated fat: 1 g ;Sodium: 136 mg

Avocado And Kiwi Green Smoothies

Servings: X
Cooking Time: X

Ingredients:

- 1 cup unsweetened apple juice
- 1 avocado, cubed
- 1 cup roughly chopped kale
- 1 kiwi, peeled and chopped
- ½ cup coconut water or water
- 2 tablespoons honey
- 1 tablespoon chopped fresh basil
- 1 tablespoon chopped fresh mint

Directions:

1. In a blender, add the apple juice, avocado, kale, kiwi, coconut water, honey, basil, and mint and blend until very smooth.
2. Pour into glasses and serve immediately.

Nutrition Info:

- Info Per Serving: Calories: 308 ; Fat:14 g ;Saturated fat: 2 g ;Sodium: 28 mg

Carrot-oatmeal Bread

Servings: 12
Cooking Time: X

Ingredients:

- 1½ cups finely chopped carrots
- 1 cup water
- 1½ cups all-purpose flour
- ¼ cup oatmeal
- 2 tablespoons oat bran
- ½ cup brown sugar
- 1/3 cup sugar
- ½ teaspoon salt
- 1 teaspoon baking powder
- ½ teaspoon baking soda
- ½ teaspoon cinnamon
- ½ teaspoon ginger
- 2/3 cup applesauce
- ¼ cup canola oil
- 2 egg whites
- ½ cup chopped walnuts

Directions:

1. Preheat oven to 350ºF. Spray a 9″ × 5″ loaf pan with nonstick cooking spray containing flour, and set aside.
2. In small saucepan, combine carrots and water and bring to a boil. Reduce heat and simmer for 5–7 minutes or until carrots are tender. Drain carrots and mash until smooth. Set aside.
3. In large bowl, combine flour, oatmeal, oat bran, brown sugar, sugar, salt, baking powder, baking soda, cinnamon, and ginger and mix well. In medium bowl combine mashed carrots, applesauce, canola oil, and egg whites, and beat well. Stir into dry ingredients until blended. Fold in walnuts.
4. Pour batter into prepared pan. Bake for 55–65 minutes or until bread is deep golden-brown and toothpick inserted in center comes out clean. Remove from pan and let cool on wire rack.

Nutrition Info:

- Info Per Serving: Calories: 241.05; Fat: 8.56 g ;Saturated fat:0.66 g ;Sodium:107.36 mg

Whole-grain Cornbread

Servings: 9
Cooking Time: X

Ingredients:
- ¼ cup all-purpose flour
- ½ cup whole-wheat flour
- ¼ cup brown sugar
- 2 teaspoons baking powder
- 1 teaspoon baking soda
- 1 cup cornmeal
- 1/3 cup oat bran
- 1 egg
- 2 egg whites
- ¼ cup honey
- 1 cup buttermilk
- ¼ cup canola oil

Directions:
1. Preheat oven to 400ºF. Spray a 9″ square pan with nonstick cooking spray containing flour, and set aside. In large mixing bowl, combine flour, whole-wheat flour, brown sugar, baking powder, baking soda, cornmeal, and oat bran and mix well.
2. In small bowl, combine egg, egg whites, honey, buttermilk, and canola oil and beat to combine. Add to dry ingredients and stir just until mixed.
3. Spoon into prepared pan and smooth top. Bake for 25–35 minutes or until bread is golden brown.

Nutrition Info:
- Info Per Serving: Calories: 252.79; Fat:7.58 g ;Saturated fat:0.87 g ;Sodium: 272.96 mg

Cashew & Berry Shake

Servings: 2
Cooking Time: 5 Min

Ingredients:
- 2 cups fresh or frozen berries (your choice)
- 1¾ cups unsweetened cashew milk
- 1 cup fresh or frozen spinach, roughly chopped
- ¼ cup cashew butter
- ½ cup ice cubes

Directions:
1. In a blender, add the berries of choice, cashew milk, spinach, and cashew butter. Blend until lump-free and smooth.
2. Add the ice cubes and blend until smooth.

Nutrition Info:
- Info Per Serving: Calories: 324 ; Fat: 22g ;Saturated fat: 1 g ;Sodium: 186 mg

Maghrebi Poached Eggs

Servings: 4
Cooking Time: 25 Min

Ingredients:
- 1 tbsp. avocado oil
- 1 medium red bell pepper, chopped
- 1 (28 oz) can low-sodium diced tomatoes
- 1 tsp ground cumin
- Fine sea salt
- Ground black pepper
- 4 large free-range eggs
- ¼ cup cilantro, chopped

Directions:
1. Heat the avocado oil in a large heavy-bottom pan over medium-high heat.
2. Add the red bell pepper and cook for 4 to 6 minutes, until softened.
3. Add the tomatoes with the juice and cumin. Cook for 10 minutes, or until the flavor comes together and the sauce has thickened. Season with salt and pepper to taste.
4. Use a large spoon to make 4 depressions in the tomato mixture. Carefully crack an egg into each depression. Cover the pan and cook for 5 to 7 minutes, or until the eggs are cooked to your liking. Remove from the heat.
5. Divide into 4 bowls and garnish with chopped cilantro. Serve while hot.

Nutrition Info:
- Info Per Serving: Calories: 146 ; Fat: 9 g ;Saturated fat: 2 g ;Sodium: 102 mg

Chocolate Pancakes

Servings: 6–8
Cooking Time: X

Ingredients:
- 1½ cups flour
- 1/3 cup sugar
- 1 teaspoon baking powder
- ½ teaspoon baking soda
- ¼ cup cocoa powder
- ½ teaspoon salt
- ¼ cup vegetable oil
- 1 egg
- 1 egg white
- ½ cup buttermilk
- 1 teaspoon vanilla
- 2 tablespoons butter or margarine

Directions:
1. In medium bowl, combine flour, sugar, baking powder, baking soda, cocoa, and salt. In small bowl, combine oil, egg, egg white, buttermilk, and vanilla and beat until blended.
2. Add wet ingredients to dry ingredients and mix just until smooth, using an eggbeater or wire whisk. Let stand for 10 minutes.
3. Heat a large griddle or frying pan over medium heat. Grease the griddle with some of the butter. Pour batter in ¼-cup portions onto griddle. Cook until the sides look dry and bubbles begin to form and break on the surface, about 3–5 minutes. Turn and cook for 1–2 minutes on second side; serve immediately.

Nutrition Info:
- Info Per Serving: Calories: 227.12; Fat: 11.05g ;Saturated fat: 3.23 g ;Sodium: 177.18 mg

Amaranth And Date Porridge

Servings: 4
Cooking Time: 22 Minutes

Ingredients:
- 1 cup amaranth
- 2½ cups water
- ½ cup unsweetened apple juice
- 1 tablespoon pure maple syrup
- 1 teaspoon canola oil
- ⅛ teaspoon ground nutmeg
- Pinch salt
- ⅓ cup Medjool dates, pitted and chopped

Directions:
1. In a medium saucepan, combine the amaranth, water, apple juice, maple syrup, canola oil, nutmeg, and salt.
2. Bring to a boil over medium heat, reduce heat to low, and simmer for 15 minutes, stirring occasionally.
3. Stir the mixture and add the dates.
4. Continue cooking for another 5 to 7 minutes, stirring frequently, or until the porridge is thickened and the amaranth is tender. Serve immediately.

Nutrition Info:
- Info Per Serving: Calories: 252; Fat: 5 g ;Saturated fat: 1 g ;Sodium: 47 mg

Roasted Garlic Bread

Servings: 32
Cooking Time: X

Ingredients:
- 1 recipe Light Whole-Grain Bread
- 2 recipes Roasted Garlic
- 2 tablespoons butter

Directions:
1. Prepare bread dough and let rise once. Punch down dough and let rest for 10 minutes. Remove cloves of garlic from papery skins, keeping cloves whole. Knead cloves into bread.
2. Divide dough in half and shape into two ovals. Grease two oval shapes on a cookie sheet and place dough on the greased spots. Cover and let rise for 1 hour, until doubled in size.
3. Preheat oven to 350°F. Bake loaves for 35–45 minutes or until golden brown. Brush each loaf with butter, then place on wire rack to cool completely.

Nutrition Info:
- Info Per Serving: Calories:156.26; Fat: 4.05 g ;Saturated fat:1.28 g ;Sodium: 92.19 mg

Cinnamon-hazelnut Scones

Servings: 8
Cooking Time: X

Ingredients:
- 1 cup all-purpose flour
- 1 cup whole-wheat flour
- 1/3 cup brown sugar
- 1 teaspoon cinnamon
- 1 teaspoon baking powder
- ½ teaspoon baking soda
- 3 tablespoons butter or plant sterol margarine
- 3 tablespoons canola oil
- 1 egg
- ½ cup buttermilk
- 1 teaspoon vanilla
- ½ cup dried cranberries
- ½ cup chopped hazelnuts
- 1 tablespoon milk

Directions:
1. Preheat oven to 400ºF. Line cookie sheet with parchment paper and set aside. In large bowl, combine flour, whole-wheat flour, brown sugar, cinnamon, baking powder, and baking soda and mix well. Cut in butter until particles are fine.
2. In small bowl, combine oil, egg, buttermilk, and vanilla and beat to combine. Add to dry ingredients and mix just until moistened.
3. Add cranberries and hazelnuts and mix just until blended. Turn out onto floured surface and toss several times to coat.
4. Pat dough into an 8″ circle on prepared cookie sheet. Cut into 8 triangles and separate slightly. Brush with milk. Bake for 15 to 18 minutes or until scones are golden brown. Cool for 5 minutes, then serve.

Nutrition Info:
- Info Per Serving: Calories:286.34 ; Fat:14.98 g ;Saturated fat:3.77 g ;Sodium:184.16 mg

Spicy Salmon Avocado Sandwich

Servings: 5
Cooking Time: X

Ingredients:
- 2 (7½-ounce) cans low-sodium, deboned salmon packed in water, drained
- ⅓ cup Spicy Honey Sauce
- 3 tablespoons low-fat plain Greek yogurt
- 5 slices whole wheat or whole-grain toast
- 1 avocado, thinly sliced

Directions:
1. In a medium bowl, mix the salmon, Spicy Honey Sauce, and Greek yogurt until well combined.
2. Scoop about 5 tablespoons of the spicy salmon mixture onto each toast slice and top with avocado slices for an open-faced sandwich. Serve immediately.

Nutrition Info:
- Info Per Serving: Calories:354 ; Fat: 18g ;Saturated fat: 2g ;Sodium: 479mg

Whole-grain Oatmeal Bread

Servings: 32
Cooking Time: X

Ingredients:
- 1 cup warm water
- 2 (¼-ounce) packages active dry yeast
- ¼ cup honey
- 1 cup skim milk
- 1 cup oatmeal
- 1 teaspoon salt
- 3 tablespoons canola oil
- 1 egg
- 1½ cups whole-wheat flour
- ½ cup medium rye flour
- ¼ cup ground flaxseed
- 3 to 4 cups bread flour
- 2 tablespoons butter

Directions:
1. In small bowl, combine water and yeast; let stand until bubbly, about 5 minutes. Meanwhile, in medium saucepan combine honey, milk, oatmeal, salt, and canola oil. Heat just until very warm (about 120ºF). Remove from heat and beat in egg. Combine in large bowl with whole-wheat flour, rye flour, flaxseed, and 1 cup bread flour. Add yeast mixture and beat for 1 minute. Cover and let rise for 30 minutes.
2. Gradually stir in enough remaining bread flour to make a firm dough. Turn onto floured surface and knead until dough is elastic, about 10 minutes. Place in greased bowl, turning to grease top. Cover and let rise for 1 hour. Punch down dough, divide in half, and form into loaves. Place in greased 9″ × 5″ loaf pans, cover, and let rise for 30 minutes.
3. Bake in preheated 350ºF oven for 25–30 minutes or until golden brown. Brush with butter, then remove to wire racks to cool.

Nutrition Info:
- Info Per Serving: Calories: 136.74; Fat:3.46 g ;Saturated fat: 0.77 g ;Sodium: 85.39 mg

Navajo Chili Bread

Servings: 12
Cooking Time: X

Ingredients:
- 3 tablespoons olive oil
- ½ cup minced onion
- 2 cloves garlic, minced
- 2 jalapeño peppers, minced
- ½ cup finely chopped red bell pepper
- 1¼ cups all-purpose flour
- 1 cup yellow cornmeal
- 1/8 teaspoon salt
- 1 teaspoon baking powder
- ½ teaspoon baking soda
- 2 teaspoons chili powder
- ½ cup liquid egg substitute
- ¼ cup buttermilk
- 2 tablespoons molasses
- ½ cup shredded Pepper Jack cheese

Directions:
1. Preheat oven to 375ºF. Spray a 9″ square glass baking dish with nonstick cooking spray containing flour, and set aside.
2. In small saucepan, heat olive oil over medium heat Add onion, garlic, jalapeño, and red bell pepper; cook and stir until crisp-tender, about 4 minutes. Remove from heat.
3. In large bowl, combine flour, cornmeal, salt, baking powder, baking soda, and chili powder, and mix to combine. Add egg substitute, buttermilk, and molasses to vegetables in saucepan, and beat to combine. Stir into flour mixture until combined, then fold in cheese.
4. Pour batter into prepared pan. Bake for 30–40 minutes or until bread is light golden-brown and toothpick inserted in center comes out clean. Let cool for 15 minutes, then serve.

Nutrition Info:
- Info Per Serving: Calories:223.97 ; Fat:7.59 g ;Saturated fat:2.11 g ;Sodium: 232.04 mg

Spinach Artichoke Pizza

Servings: 8
Cooking Time: X

Ingredients:
- 1 (10-ounce) package frozen chopped spinach, thawed and drained
- 1 (9-ounce) package frozen artichoke hearts, thawed and drained
- 1 tablespoon olive oil
- 1 onion, chopped
- 3 cloves garlic, minced
- 1 red bell pepper, chopped
- 1 (8-ounce) package sliced mushrooms
- 1 cup part-skim ricotta cheese
- ¼ cup grated Parmesan cheese
- 1 cup shredded part-skim mozzarella cheese
- ½ cup shredded extra-sharp Cheddar cheese
- 1 Whole-Grain Pizza Crust

Directions:
1. Preheat oven to 400ºF. Press spinach between paper towels to remove all excess moisture. Cut artichoke hearts into small pieces.
2. In large saucepan, heat olive oil. Cook onion, garlic, red pepper, and mushrooms until crisp-tender, about 4 minutes. Add spinach; cook and stir until liquid evaporates, about 5 minutes longer. Add mushrooms; cook and stir for 2–3 minutes longer.
3. Drain vegetable mixture if necessary. Place in medium bowl and let cool for 20 minutes. Then blend in ricotta and Parmesan cheeses.
4. Spread on pizza crust. Top with mozzarella and Cheddar cheeses. Bake for 20–25 minutes or until pizza is hot and cheese is melted and begins to brown. Serve immediately.

Nutrition Info:
- Info Per Serving: Calories: 335.56; Fat:13.05 g ;Saturated fat: 6.06 g ;Sodium: 317.04 mg

Cornmeal-cranberry Rolls

Servings: 18
Cooking Time: X

Ingredients:
- ½ cup buttermilk
- ½ cup water
- ½ cup yellow cornmeal
- 1/3 cup canola oil
- 2½ to 3½ cups all-purpose flour
- 1 (¼-ounce) package instant-blend dried yeast
- ½ teaspoon salt
- 1 egg
- 2 egg whites
- 1/3 cup honey
- 2/3 cup chopped dried cranberries
- 2 tablespoons butter, melted

Directions:
1. In medium saucepan, combine buttermilk, water, cornmeal, and oil over medium heat. Cook, stirring, until very warm. Remove from heat.
2. In large bowl, combine 2 cups flour, yeast, and salt and mix well. Add the buttermilk mixture along with egg, egg whites, and honey. Beat for 2 minutes. Then gradually add enough remaining flour until a stiff batter forms. Stir in cranberries.
3. Cover and let rise until doubled, about 1 hour. Grease 18 muffin cups with nonstick cooking spray. Spoon batter into the prepared cups, filling each full. Cover and let rise for 30 minutes.
4. Preheat oven to 350ºF. Bake rolls for 20–30 minutes or until golden brown and set. Immediately brush with butter. Remove from pans and let cool on wire racks.

Nutrition Info:
- Info Per Serving: Calories: 194.31; Fat:6.20 g ;Saturated fat: 1.37g ;Sodium:113.41 mg

Cranberry-orange Bread

Servings: 12
Cooking Time: X

Ingredients:
- ¼ cup orange juice
- 2 tablespoons frozen orange juice concentrate, thawed
- ½ teaspoon almond extract
- ¼ cup canola oil
- 1 egg
- 1/3 cup sugar
- ½ cup brown sugar
- 1 teaspoon grated orange zest
- 1½ cups all-purpose flour
- ¼ cup whole-wheat flour
- 1 teaspoon baking soda
- 1 teaspoon baking powder
- 2 cups chopped cranberries
- ½ cup chopped hazelnuts

Directions:
1. Preheat oven to 350ºF. Spray a 9″ × 5″ loaf pan with nonstick cooking spray containing flour, and set aside.
2. In medium bowl, combine orange juice, orange juice concentrate, almond extract, canola oil, egg, sugar, brown sugar, and orange zest and beat to combine.
3. In large bowl, combine flour, whole-wheat flour, baking soda, baking powder, and mix. Make a well in the center of the flour mixture and pour in the orange juice mixture. Stir just until dry ingredients are moistened.
4. Fold in cranberries and hazelnuts. Pour into prepared pan. Bake for 55–65 minutes or until bread is golden-brown and toothpick inserted in center comes out clean. Remove from pan and let cool on wire rack.

Nutrition Info:
- Info Per Serving: Calories: 232.48; Fat: 8.24 g ;Saturated fat:0.72g ;Sodium: 145.81 mg

Blueberry Breakfast Muffins

Servings: 9
Cooking Time: 20 Minutes

Ingredients:
- Olive oil
- 2 bananas
- 1 cup steel-cut oats
- 1 large egg
- 1 teaspoon baking powder
- ½ cup fresh blueberries

Directions:
1. Preheat the oven to 350°F. Lightly grease 9 cups of a muffin tin with oil.
2. In a medium bowl, mash the bananas with a fork until smooth.
3. Mix in the oats, egg, and baking powder until well combined.
4. Gently fold the blueberries into the mixture.
5. Equally divide the batter into the 9 prepared muffin cups and bake for 20 minutes, or until a toothpick inserted in the center comes out clean.
6. Remove the muffins from the oven and let them cool for 10 minutes before serving.

Nutrition Info:
- Info Per Serving: Calories: 112; Fat: 2g ;Saturated fat: 0g ;Sodium: 9mg

Nutty Quinoa Waffles

Servings: 4
Cooking Time: 15 Minutes

Ingredients:
- 1 cup quinoa flour
- 1½ teaspoons baking powder
- 1 teaspoon ground cinnamon
- ⅛ teaspoon ground nutmeg
- Pinch salt
- 1 egg, separated
- ½ cup almond or soy milk
- 2 tablespoons honey or pure maple syrup
- 1 teaspoon vanilla extract
- 3 tablespoons ground pecans

Directions:
1. In a medium bowl, combine the quinoa flour, baking powder, cinnamon, nutmeg, and salt and blend well with a wire whisk or fork.
2. In a small bowl, combine the egg yolk, almond milk, honey, and vanilla and mix well.
3. In another medium bowl, beat the egg white until stiff.
4. Stir the egg yolk mixture into the dry ingredients, then fold in the egg white.
5. Preheat a waffle iron and spray it with nonstick cooking spray.
6. Add batter to the waffle iron per the manufacturer's instructions. Close the iron and cook until the steaming stops, 4 to 5 minutes. Remove the waffle from the iron, sprinkle with ground pecans, and serve immediately.

Nutrition Info:
- Info Per Serving: Calories: 195 ; Fat: 7 g ;Saturated fat: 1 g ;Sodium: 169 mg

Orange-vanilla Smoothie

Servings: 2
Cooking Time: X

Ingredients:
- 1½ cups orange yogurt
- ½ cup orange juice
- 1 orange, peeled and sliced
- ¼ cup vanilla-flavored whey protein
- 1 teaspoon vanilla
- 4 ice cubes

Directions:
1. Place yogurt, orange juice, orange, whey protein, and vanilla in blender or food processor; blend or process until smooth. Add ice cubes; blend or process until thick. Pour into glasses and serve immediately.

Nutrition Info:
- Info Per Serving: Calories: 346.91; Fat: 2.34 g ;Saturated fat: 1.22 gr;Sodium: 241.12 mg

Hot Pepper And Salsa Frittata

Servings: 3
Cooking Time: X

Ingredients:
- 2 tablespoons olive oil
- ½ cup finely chopped red onion
- 1 jalapeño pepper, minced
- ½ cup egg substitute
- 4 egg whites
- ¼ cup skim milk
- 3 tablespoons grated Parmesan cheese
- ½ cup Super Spicy Salsa (page 85)
- 2 tablespoons chopped cilantro

Directions:
1. In large nonstick skillet, heat olive oil over medium heat. Add onion and jalapeño pepper; cook and stir until crisp-tender, about 4 minutes.
2. Meanwhile, in medium bowl beat egg substitute, egg whites, milk, and cheese until combined. Pour into skillet. Cook, running spatula around edge of frittata as it cooks, until eggs are soft set and light brown on the bottom.
3. Preheat broiler. Place frittata 6″ from heat and broil for 4–7 minutes, watching carefully, until the top is browned and set. Top with salsa and cilantro and serve immediately.

Nutrition Info:
- Info Per Serving: Calories: 201.08;Fat: 201.08 ;Saturated fat: 2.67 g;Sodium: 289.79 mg

Protein Cereal

Servings: 4
Cooking Time: 20 Min

Ingredients:
- 1¾ cups water
- 1 cup quinoa
- Pinch fine sea salt
- 1 cup raisins
- ½ cup almonds, roughly chopped
- 1 cup unsweetened almond milk
- 4 tsp organic honey

Directions:
1. In a medium stockpot, add the water, quinoa, and salt, allow to boil.
2. Bring the heat down to low and simmer, covered, for 15 minutes, or until the water is absorbed. Remove from the heat and let it rest for 5 minutes.
3. Add the raisins and almonds, mix to combine.
4. Place a ¾ cup of the quinoa mixture into 4 bowls and pour a ¼ cup of almond milk in each bowl. Drizzle each bowl of quinoa with 1 tsp of organic honey.

Nutrition Info:
- Info Per Serving: Calories: 313 ; Fat: 10 g ;Saturated fat: 1 g ;Sodium: 33 mg

Pork And Beef Mains

Pork And Beef Mains

Beef-risotto–stuffed Peppers

Servings: 4
Cooking Time: X

Ingredients:
- 1 tablespoon olive oil
- 1 onion, chopped
- 2 cups Beef Risotto
- 1 egg
- 1 egg white
- 1 tomato, chopped
- 2 slices Whole-Grain Oatmeal Bread
- 4 bell peppers
- 1 cup Spaghetti Sauce
- ¼ cup water

Directions:
1. Preheat oven to 350ºF. Spray a 9"-square baking pan with nonstick cooking spray and set aside. In medium saucepan, heat olive oil over medium heat. Add onion; cook and stir until tender, about 5 minutes. Remove from heat and stir in risotto, egg, egg white, and tomato and mix well.
2. Make crumbs from the bread and add to the risotto mixture. Cut off the pepper tops and remove membranes and seeds. Stuff with risotto mixture.
3. Place stuffed peppers in prepared baking dish. In small bowl, combine Spaghetti Sauce and water; pour over and around peppers. Cover with foil and bake for 45–55 minutes or until peppers are tender. Serve immediately.

Nutrition Info:
- Info Per Serving: Calories: 331.74; Fat:12.15 g ;Saturated fat:3.20g ;Sodium:130.25 mg

Fruit-stuffed Pork Tenderloin

Servings: 6
Cooking Time: X

Ingredients:
- 1½ pounds pork tenderloin
- ¼ cup dry white wine
- 6 prunes, chopped
- 5 dried apricots, chopped
- 1 onion, chopped
- 2 tablespoons flour
- 1/8 teaspoon salt
- 1/8 teaspoon pepper
- 2 tablespoons olive oil
- ½ cup Low-Sodium Chicken Broth
- 1 teaspoon dried thyme leaves

Directions:
1. Trim excess fat from meat. Cut tenderloin lengthwise, cutting to, but not through, the other side. Open up the meat and place on work surface, cut side up. Lightly pound with a rolling pin or meat mallet until about ½" thick.
2. In small saucepan, combine wine, prunes, apricots, and onion. Simmer for 10 minutes or until fruit is soft and wine is absorbed. Place this mixture in the center of the pork tenderloin. Roll the pork around the fruit mixture, using a toothpick to secure.
3. Sprinkle pork with flour, salt, and pepper. In ovenproof saucepan, heat olive oil. Add pork; brown on all sides, turning frequently, about 5–6 minutes. Add broth and thyme to saucepan. Bake for 25–35 minutes or until internal temperature registers 155ºF. Let pork stand for 5 minutes, remove toothpicks, and slice to serve.

Nutrition Info:
- Info Per Serving: Calories: 249.06 ; Fat: 9.82 g ;Saturated fat: 2.41 g ;Sodium: 102.85 mg

Whole-wheat Spaghetti And Meatballs

Servings: 6–8
Cooking Time: X

Ingredients:
- 1 recipe Sirloin Meatballs in Sauce
- 1 (8-ounce) can no-salt tomato sauce
- ½ cup grated carrots
- 1 (16-ounce) package whole-wheat spaghetti
- ½ cup grated Parmesan cheese, divided

Directions:
1. Bring a large pot of water to a boil. Prepare the Sirloin Meatballs in Sauce, adding tomato sauce and grated carrots to the sauce. Simmer until meatballs are cooked.
2. Cook spaghetti in water according to package directions or until almost al dente. Drain spaghetti, reserving ¼ cup cooking water. Add spaghetti to meatballs in sauce along with ¼ cup of the cheese. Simmer, stirring gently, for 5–6 minutes or until pasta is al dente, adding reserved cooking water if necessary for desired sauce consistency. Sprinkle with the remaining ¼ cup Parmesan cheese and serve immediately.

Nutrition Info:
- Info Per Serving: Calories: 386.78; Fat:12.34 g ;Saturated fat: 4.08 g ;Sodium: 444.23 mg

Classic Spaghetti And Meatballs

Servings: X
Cooking Time: 20 Minutes

Ingredients:
- Nonstick olive oil cooking spray
- 6 ounces extra-lean ground beef
- 1 large egg white
- ¼ cup ground almonds
- 2 teaspoons chopped fresh parsley
- ¼ teaspoon garlic powder
- Pinch sea salt
- Pinch freshly ground black pepper
- 2 cups Double Tomato Sauce or your favorite low-sodium marinara sauce
- 4 ounces dry spaghetti

Directions:
1. Preheat the oven to 400°F.
2. Line a baking sheet with parchment paper and spray it lightly with cooking spray. Set aside.
3. In a medium bowl, combine the ground beef, egg white, almonds, parsley, garlic powder, salt, and pepper until well mixed. Form the meat mixture into 12 meatballs and spread out on the baking sheet.
4. Bake the meatballs until cooked through, about 20 minutes. Remove from the oven and set aside.
5. While the meatballs are cooking, warm the sauce in a medium saucepan over medium heat. Cook the spaghetti according to package instructions.
6. Drain the pasta and serve topped with sauce and meatballs.

Nutrition Info:
- Info Per Serving: Calories: 574 ; Fat: 12 g ;Saturated fat: 2 g ;Sodium: 443 mg

Mini Lasagna Cups

Servings: 3
Cooking Time: 18 Minutes

Ingredients:
- ⅓ pound 98% lean ground beef
- 2 scallions, minced
- 3 cloves garlic, minced
- 1¼ cups low-sodium marinara sauce
- 1 teaspoon dried Italian seasoning
- ¾ cup low-fat ricotta cheese
- ¼ cup grated Romano cheese
- 6 (4-inch) corn tortillas

Directions:
1. Preheat the oven to 375°F. Spray 6 standard muffin cups with nonstick cooking spray and set aside.
2. In a medium nonstick skillet, sauté the ground beef with the scallions and garlic over medium-high heat, stirring to break up the meat, until the beef is browned, about 3 minutes. Drain if necessary.
3. Stir the marinara sauce and Italian seasoning into the beef mixture. Remove from the heat, then cut the corn tortillas into thirds.
4. Dip a piece of tortilla into the meat sauce and put it into a muffin cup. Top with 2 tablespoons meat sauce. Top with one corn tortilla piece. Top with two tablespoons ricotta cheese. Add another tortilla piece, then 2 tablespoons meat sauce. Sprinkle with the Romano cheese. Repeat, filling the remaining 5 muffin cups.
5. Bake the lasagna cups for 10 to 15 minutes or until the cups are bubbling and the cheese on top is lightly browned. Transfer the muffin tin to a cooling rack.
6. Let stand for 5 minutes, then run a knife around the edges of each muffin cup and remove the mini lasagnas.

Nutrition Info:
- Info Per Serving: Calories: 266 ; Fat: 10 g ;Saturated fat: 4 g ;Sodium: 357 mg

Wasabi-roasted Filet Mignon

Servings: 12
Cooking Time: X

Ingredients:
- 1 (3-pound) filet mignon roast
- ¼ teaspoon pepper
- 1 teaspoon powdered wasabi
- 2 tablespoons sesame oil
- 2 tablespoons soy sauce

Directions:
1. Preheat oven to 400ºF. If the roast has a thin end and a thick end, fold the thin end under so the roast is about the same thickness. Place on roasting pan.
2. In small bowl, combine pepper, wasabi, oil, and soy sauce, and mix well. Brush half over roast. Roast the beef for 30 minutes, then remove and brush with remaining wasabi mixture. Return to oven for 5–10 minutes longer or until meat thermometer registers at least 145ºF for medium rare.
3. Remove from oven, cover, and let stand for 15 minutes before slicing to serve.

Nutrition Info:
- Info Per Serving: Calories:298.15; Fat: 24.00g ;Saturated fat:8.99 g ;Sodium: 143.07 mg

Pork Chops With Smoky Barbecue Rub

Servings: X
Cooking Time: 15 Minutes

Ingredients:
- 2 (6-ounce) boneless pork top-loin chops
- 2 tablespoons Smoky Barbecue Rub
- 1 teaspoon chopped fresh cilantro, for garnish

Directions:
1. Preheat a grill to medium-high heat.
2. Season the pork all over with the rub.
3. Grill the pork until it is just cooked through, turning once, about 8 minutes per side.
4. Serve topped with cilantro.

Nutrition Info:
- Info Per Serving: Calories: 287 ; Fat: 17 g ;Saturated fat: 6 g ;Sodium: 513 mg

Beef With Mushroom Kabobs

Servings: 4
Cooking Time: X

Ingredients:
- ¼ cup dry red wine
- 1 tablespoon olive oil
- 1/8 teaspoon salt
- 1/8 teaspoon cayenne pepper
- 1 tablespoon dried basil leaves
- 2 cloves garlic, minced
- 1 pound beef sirloin steak
- ½ pound button mushrooms
- ½ pound cremini mushrooms
- 1 tablespoon lemon juice

Directions:
1. In medium glass bowl, combine wine, olive oil, salt, pepper, basil leaves, and garlic, and mix well. Cut steak into 1½" cubes and add to wine mixture. Stir to coat, cover, and refrigerate for 1 hour.
2. When ready to cook, prepare and preheat grill. Drain steak, reserving marinade. Trim mushroom stems and discard; brush mushrooms with lemon juice. Thread steak and mushrooms onto metal skewers.
3. Grill for 7–10 minutes, turning once and brushing with marinade, until beef is deep golden brown and mushrooms are tender. Discard remaining marinade.

Nutrition Info:
- Info Per Serving: Calories:215.70; Fat: 7.08 g ;Saturated fat:2.39 g;Sodium: 101.33 mg

Pan-seared Beef Tenderloin With Wild Mushrooms

Servings: X
Cooking Time: 25 Minutes

Ingredients:
- 2 (4-ounce) beef tenderloin steaks, fat trimmed
- Sea salt
- Freshly ground black pepper
- Nonstick olive oil cooking spray
- 1 tablespoon canola oil
- 1 teaspoon minced garlic
- 4 cups thinly sliced wild mushrooms (shiitake, oyster, portobello, and chanterelles)
- ½ teaspoon chopped fresh thyme

Directions:
1. Season the steaks lightly with salt and pepper.
2. Lightly coat a large skillet with cooking spray and place it over medium heat. Sear the steaks until they reach your desired doneness, 5 minutes per side for medium.
3. Remove the steaks and set aside.
4. Add the canola oil to the skillet and sauté the garlic until softened, about 3 minutes.
5. Add the mushrooms and cook, stirring occasionally, until lightly caramelized, 7 to 8 minutes.
6. Stir in the thyme and season with salt and pepper.
7. Serve the steaks with the mushrooms.

Nutrition Info:
- Info Per Serving: Calories: 267 ; Fat: 15 g ;Saturated fat: 3 g ;Sodium: 72 mg

Bbq Pork Chops

Servings: 8
Cooking Time: X

Ingredients:

- 2 tablespoons olive oil
- 1 onion, chopped
- 4 cloves garlic, minced
- 1 (14-ounce) can no-salt crushed tomatoes, undrained
- 1 cup low-sodium chili sauce
- 1 tablespoon lemon juice
- 2 tablespoons mustard
- ¼ cup brown sugar
- 2 tablespoons molasses
- ½ teaspoon cumin
- 1 teaspoon dried thyme leaves
- 1/8 teaspoon ground cloves
- 8 (3-ounce) boneless pork chops

Directions:

1. In large pot, heat olive oil over medium heat. Add onion and garlic; cook and stir for 3–4 minutes until crisp-tender. Add tomatoes, chili sauce, lemon juice, mustard, sugar, molasses, cumin, thyme, and cloves. Bring to a simmer, then reduce heat, cover, and simmer for 2 hours.
2. When ready to cook, prepare and preheat grill. Spray grill rack with nonstick cooking spray and add pork chops. Grill until the chops can be easily moved, about 4 minutes. Turn and brush with sauce. Cook for 3–5 minutes longer or until chops are just pink, turning again and brushing with more sauce. Serve with sauce that hasn't been used to brush the pork.

Nutrition Info:

- Info Per Serving: Calories:276.23 ; Fat:11.80 g ;Saturated fat: 3.53 g ;Sodium: 417.98 mg

Beef Rollups With Pesto

Servings: 6
Cooking Time: X

Ingredients:

- ½ cup packed basil leaves
- ½ cup packed baby spinach leaves
- 3 cloves garlic, minced
- 1/3 cup toasted chopped hazelnuts
- 1/8 teaspoon white pepper
- 2 tablespoons grated Parmesan cheese
- 2 tablespoons olive oil
- 2 tablespoons water
- 3 tablespoons flour
- ½ teaspoon paprika
- 6 (4-ounce) top round steaks, ¼" thick
- 2 oil-packed sun-dried tomatoes, minced
- 1 tablespoon canola oil
- 1 cup Low-Sodium Beef Broth

Directions:

1. In blender or food processor, combine basil, spinach, garlic, hazelnuts, and white pepper, and blend or process until finely chopped. Add Parmesan and blend again. Add olive oil and blend until a paste forms, then add water and blend.
2. On shallow plate, combine flour, and paprika and mix well. Place beef between sheets of waxed paper and pound until ¼" thick. Spread pesto on one side of the pounded beef and sprinkle with tomatoes. Roll up, fastening closed with toothpicks.
3. Dredge rollups in flour mixture. Heat canola oil in large saucepan and brown rollups on all sides, about 5 minutes total. Pour beef broth into pan and bring to a simmer. Cover, reduce heat to low, and simmer for 40–50 minutes or until beef is tender.

Nutrition Info:

- Info Per Serving: Calories: 290.23 ; Fat:18.73g ;Saturated fat:3.90 g ;Sodium:95.79 mg

Honeyed Pork Tenderloin With Butternut Squash

Servings: X
Cooking Time: 35 Minutes

Ingredients:
- Nonstick olive oil cooking spray
- 1 (8-ounce) pork tenderloin, fat trimmed
- Sea salt
- Freshly ground black pepper
- 1 tablespoon honey
- Dash ground cloves
- 2 teaspoons canola oil, divided
- 4 cups diced butternut squash
- ¼ teaspoon chopped fresh thyme

Directions:
1. Preheat the oven to 425°F.
2. Line a baking sheet with foil and lightly spray it with cooking spray.
3. Lightly season the pork with salt and pepper and rub the meat with the honey. Sprinkle with cloves.
4. In a small skillet, heat 1 teaspoon canola oil and brown the tenderloin on all sides, about 5 minutes.
5. Place the tenderloin on the baking sheet.
6. In a medium bowl, toss the butternut squash, remaining 1 teaspoon canola oil, and thyme until well mixed.
7. Spread the squash around the tenderloin and lightly season the vegetables with salt and pepper.
8. Place the baking sheet in the oven and roast until the meat is cooked through and the squash is tender, 25 to 30 minutes.
9. Serve.

Nutrition Info:
- Info Per Serving: Calories: 310 ; Fat: 8 g ;Saturated fat: 1 g ;Sodium: 92 mg

Filet Mignon With Vegetables

Servings: 8–10
Cooking Time: X

Ingredients:
- 1 (16-ounce) package baby carrots, halved lengthwise
- 1 (8-ounce) package frozen pearl onions
- 16 new potatoes, halved
- 2 tablespoons olive oil
- 2 pounds filet mignon
- 1/8 teaspoon salt
- 1/8 teaspoon white pepper
- ½ cup dry red wine

Directions:
1. Preheat oven to 425ºF. Place carrots, onions, and potatoes in large roasting pan and drizzle with olive oil; toss to coat. Spread in an even layer. Roast for 15 minutes, then remove from oven.
2. Top with filet mignon; sprinkle the meat with salt and pepper. Pour wine over meat and vegetables.
3. Return to oven; roast for 20–30 minutes longer until beef registers 150ºF for medium. Remove from oven, tent with foil, and let stand for 5 minutes, then carve to serve.

Nutrition Info:
- Info Per Serving: Calories:442.64 ; Fat:11.83 g ;Saturated fat:3.77 g ;Sodium:140.70 mg

Servings: 4
Cooking Time: 10 Minutes

Ingredients:
- 1 fennel bulb
- 1½ cups low-sodium chicken broth
- 1 tablespoon rice wine vinegar
- 1 tablespoon honey
- 2 tablespoons cornstarch
- 1 teaspoon soy sauce
- 12 ounces boneless top loin pork chops
- Pinch salt
- ⅛ teaspoon white pepper
- 2 teaspoons olive oil
- 8 ounces cremini mushrooms, sliced
- 3 stalks celery, sliced
- 2 cloves garlic, minced

Directions:
1. To prepare the fennel, trim the root end and cut off the stalk. Cut the bulb in half and peel off the outer skin. Slice the fennel thinly crosswise, and set aside. Finely slice the stalks, if desired. Cut some of the fennel fronds into tiny pieces with kitchen scissors, and set aside.
2. In a small bowl, combine the chicken broth, rice wine vinegar, honey, cornstarch, and soy sauce, and whisk to combine. Set aside.
3. Trim excess fat from the pork chops, and cut into 1-inch pieces. Sprinkle with the salt and white pepper.
4. Heat the olive oil in a large nonstick skillet or wok over medium-high heat. Add the pork and stir-fry until lightly browned, about 3 minutes. Remove the pork to a clean plate.
5. Add the fennel, fennel stalks if using, mushrooms, celery, and garlic to the skillet, and stir-fry for 3 to 4 minutes or until crisp-tender.
6. Stir the broth mixture, add it to the skillet, and bring to a simmer.
7. Add the pork and stir-fry 2 to 3 minutes or until the pork is cooked to at least 150°F on a meat thermometer and the sauce is thickened. Sprinkle with the reserved fennel fronds and serve immediately.

Nutrition Info:
- Info Per Serving: Calories: 204 ; Fat: 7 g ;Saturated fat: 2 g ;Sodium: 324 mg

Pork Skewers With Cherry Tomatoes

Servings: 4
Cooking Time: X

Ingredients:
- ¼ pound pork tenderloin, cubed
- 24 cherry tomatoes
- 1 onion, cut into eighths
- 2 tablespoons olive oil
- 1 tablespoon lemon juice
- 1/8 teaspoon pepper
- 2 tablespoons chopped flat-leaf parsley
- 1 tablespoon fresh oregano leaves
- ¼ cup shredded Parmesan cheese

Directions:
1. Prepare and preheat grill. Thread pork, cherry tomatoes, and onion on metal skewers. In small bowl, combine olive oil, lemon juice, pepper, parsley, and oregano leaves. Brush skewers with olive oil mixture.
2. Grill skewers 6″ from medium coals for 8–10 minutes, turning and brushing occasionally with marinade, until pork registers 155ºF. Sprinkle with Parmesan, let stand to melt, and serve.

Nutrition Info:
- Info Per Serving: Calories:240.01; Fat: 10.48 g ;Saturated fat: 3.50 g ;Sodium:177.18 mg

Western Omelet

Servings: 4
Cooking Time: X

Ingredients:
- 1 tablespoon olive oil
- ½ cup chopped onion
- 3 cloves garlic, minced
- ½ cup chopped green bell pepper
- ½ cup chopped red bell pepper
- 3 ounces chopped ham
- 1 egg
- 8 egg whites
- ¼ teaspoon cayenne pepper
- 1 teaspoon chili powder
- ¼ cup skim milk
- 1/8 teaspoon pepper

Directions:
1. In large nonstick skillet, heat olive oil over medium heat. Add onion, garlic, and bell peppers; cook and stir until crisp-tender, about 4 minutes. Add ham; cook and stir until ham is hot.
2. In large bowl, combine egg, egg whites, cayenne pepper, chili powder, milk, and pepper and mix well. Pour into skillet with vegetables and ham.
3. Cook, running a spatula around the edges to let uncooked mixture flow underneath, until eggs are set and bottom is golden brown. Fold omelet over on itself and slide onto plate, serve.

Nutrition Info:
- Info Per Serving: Calories: 216.81; Fat:13.12g ;Saturated fat: 5.15 g ;Sodium: 477.02 mg

Beef And Broccoli

Servings: 4
Cooking Time: 10 Minutes

Ingredients:
- ½ pound top sirloin steak
- ⅛ teaspoon cayenne pepper
- ¼ teaspoon ground ginger
- 1¼ cups low-sodium beef broth
- 1 tablespoon honey
- 2 tablespoons cornstarch
- 1 teaspoon hoisin sauce
- 1 teaspoon low-sodium soy sauce
- 1 teaspoon olive oil
- 1 onion, chopped
- 3 cloves garlic, minced
- 3 cups broccoli florets

Directions:
1. Trim any visible fat from the steak. Cut the steak into ½-inch strips. Place in a bowl, sprinkle with the cayenne pepper and ginger, and toss. Set aside.
2. In a small bowl, thoroughly combine the beef broth, honey, cornstarch, hoisin sauce, and soy sauce. Set aside.
3. In a large nonstick skillet or wok, heat the olive oil over medium-high heat.
4. Add the steak strips in a single layer, and cook for 1 minute. Turn the steak and cook for 1 minute longer. Transfer the steak to a plate.
5. Add the onion and garlic to the skillet, and stir-fry for 2 minutes.
6. Add the broccoli, and stir-fry for 2 minutes.
7. Add the broth mixture and bring to a simmer. Simmer for 1 to 2 minutes or until the sauce has thickened.
8. Return the beef to the skillet, and stir-fry for 1 minute. Serve immediately.

Nutrition Info:
- Info Per Serving: Calories: 204 ; Fat:9 g ;Saturated fat: 3g ;Sodium: 141 mg

Pork Chops With Mustard Sauce

Servings: 4
Cooking Time: X

Ingredients:
- 2 tablespoons Dijon mustard, divided
- 2 tablespoons plain yogurt
- 1/8 teaspoon pepper
- 4 (3-ounce) bone-in pork chops
- 2 tablespoons olive oil
- 1 onion, chopped
- 1 tablespoon flour
- 1 cup Low-Sodium Chicken Broth
- ¼ cup dry white wine

Directions:

1. Prepare and preheat grill. In small bowl, combine 1 tablespoon mustard, yogurt, and pepper and mix well. Spread mixture on both sides of pork chops; set aside for 15 minutes.
2. In small saucepan, heat olive oil over medium heat. Add onion; cook and stir until tender, about 5 minutes. Add flour; cook and stir until combined and bubbly. Add broth, wine, and remaining 1 tablespoon mustard; bring to a boil, stirring with wire whisk, until sauce is slightly thickened.
3. Grill the chops for 4–6 minutes on each side, turning once, until pork is just slightly pink in the center. Serve with the sauce.

Nutrition Info:
- Info Per Serving: Calories:284.17 ; Fat:17.76 g ;Saturated fat:4.69 g ;Sodium: 141.49 mg

Beef Burrito Skillet

Servings: 4
Cooking Time: 15 Minutes

Ingredients:
- ¾ pound extra-lean ground beef
- 1 onion, chopped
- 4 cloves garlic, minced
- 1 jalapeño pepper, seeded and minced
- 1 tablespoon chili powder
- ½ teaspoon cumin
- 1 (16-ounce) can no-salt-added pinto beans, rinsed and drained
- 1 tomato, chopped
- 1 cup frozen corn, thawed
- ½ cup low-sodium salsa
- 3 corn tortillas, cut into 1-inch strips
- 2 tablespoons crumbled cotija cheese
- ¼ cup low-fat sour cream

Directions:

1. In a large skillet, sauté the ground beef, onion, garlic, and jalapeño pepper, stirring to break up the meat, until the beef is browned, about 5 to 7 minutes.
2. Add the chili powder and cumin, and stir.
3. Add in the pinto beans, tomato, corn, and salsa, and bring to a simmer. Simmer for 5 minutes, stirring occasionally.
4. Stir in the corn tortillas and cook for 3 to 4 minutes. Top with the cheese and sour cream, and serve.

Nutrition Info:
- Info Per Serving: Calories: 403 ; Fat: 10 g ;Saturated fat: 4 g ;Sodium: 215 mg

Grilled Coffee-rubbed Sirloin Steak

Servings: X
Cooking Time: 15 Minutes

Ingredients:
- 1 tablespoon espresso coffee powder
- 1½ teaspoons dark brown sugar
- 1 teaspoon smoky paprika
- ½ teaspoon chili powder
- ¼ teaspoon garlic powder
- ¼ teaspoon ground black pepper
- ¼ teaspoon salt
- 1 (10-ounce) sirloin steak, trimmed to ⅛-inch fat

Directions:
1. In a small bowl, stir together the espresso powder, sugar, paprika, chili powder, garlic powder, pepper, and salt.
2. Rub the coffee mixture all over the steak.
3. Preheat the grill to medium-high.
4. Grill the steak, turning once, until it is the desired doneness, about 7 minutes per side for medium (160°F).
5. Transfer the steak to a cutting board and let rest for at least 10 minutes before slicing it against the grain.
6. Serve.

Nutrition Info:
- Info Per Serving: Calories: 285 ; Fat: 18 g ;Saturated fat: 7 g ;Sodium: 274 mg

Stir-fried Crispy Orange Beef

Servings: 4
Cooking Time: 12 Minutes

Ingredients:
- ½ cup low-sodium beef broth, divided
- 3 tablespoons orange juice
- 1 teaspoon fresh orange zest
- 1 teaspoon low-sodium soy sauce
- 1 teaspoon Thai chili paste
- 2 tablespoons rice flour or cornstarch, divided
- ½ pound top round steak
- 1 teaspoon paprika
- ⅛ teaspoon cayenne pepper
- 1 teaspoon olive oil
- 3 scallions, chopped
- 2 cups snow pea pods
- 1 red bell pepper, seeded and chopped
- 1 carrot, grated

Directions:
1. In a small bowl, combine all but 1 tablespoon of the beef broth, the orange juice, orange zest, soy sauce, Thai chili paste, and 1 tablespoon of the rice flour or cornstarch, and mix well. Set aside.
2. Trim off the fat from the steak and discard. Slice into thin strips and put in a medium bowl. Add the remaining 1 tablespoon rice flour or cornstarch, the paprika, and cayenne pepper to the beef and toss to coat.
3. Heat ½ teaspoon of the olive oil in a nonstick skillet or wok over high heat.
4. Add half the beef strips in a single layer. Let them cook for 2 minutes, then turn and cook for 2 to 3 minutes or until the beef is crisp. Remove the beef to a clean plate.
5. Repeat with remaining ½ teaspoon olive oil and beef strips. Remove the beef to the plate.
6. Reduce the heat to medium high. Add reserved 1 tablespoon beef broth to the skillet, then add the scallions, pea pods, and carrots. Stir-fry for 2 to 3 minutes, or until the vegetables are crisp-tender.
7. Add the orange–beef broth mixture to the skillet and stir-fry for 1 to 2 minutes or until the sauce has thickened slightly. Add the beef strips, and stir-fry for 1 minute.

Nutrition Info:
- Info Per Serving: Calories: 175 ; Fat: 4 g ;Saturated fat: 1 g ;Sodium: 194 mg

Pork Scallops With Spinach

Servings: 6
Cooking Time: X

Ingredients:
- 3 tablespoons flour
- 1/8 teaspoon salt
- 1/8 teaspoon pepper
- 6 (3-ounce) pork scallops
- 2 tablespoons olive oil
- 1 onion, chopped
- 1 (10-ounce) package frozen chopped spinach, thawed
- 1 tablespoon flour
- ½ teaspoon celery seed
- 1/3 cup nonfat light cream
- 1/3 cup part-skim ricotta cheese
- ½ cup dried breadcrumbs, divided
- 2 tablespoons grated Romano cheese

Directions:
1. Preheat oven to 350ºF. On plate, combine 3 tablespoons flour, salt, and pepper and mix well. Pound pork scallops, if necessary, to A1/8" thickness.
2. Heat olive oil in nonstick pan over medium-high heat. Dredge pork in flour mixture and sauté in pan, turning once, until just browned, about 1 minute per side. Remove to a baking dish.
3. Add onion to pan; cook and stir for 3 minutes. Drain spinach well and add to pan; cook and stir until liquid evaporates. Add flour and celery seed; cook and stir for 1 minute.
4. Stir in light cream; cook and stir until thickened, about 3 minutes. Remove from heat and add ricotta cheese and half of the breadcrumbs.
5. Divide spinach mixture on top of pork in baking dish. Top with remaining breadcrumbs and Romano. Bake for 10–15 minutes or until pork is tender and thoroughly cooked. Serve immediately.

Nutrition Info:
- Info Per Serving: Calories: 298.66; Fat: 12.60 g ;Saturated fat:4.08 g ;Sodium: 303.25 mg

Meatball Pizza

Servings: 6
Cooking Time: X

Ingredients:
- 1 Whole-Grain Pizza Crust , prebaked
- 1 tablespoon olive oil
- 1 onion, chopped
- 1 green bell pepper, chopped
- ½ cup shredded carrots
- 1 (6-ounce) can no-salt tomato paste
- 2 tablespoons mustard
- ¼ cup water
- 12 plain Sirloin Meatballs , baked
- 1 cup shredded extra-sharp Cheddar cheese
- ½ cup shredded part-skim mozzarella cheese

Directions:
1. Preheat oven to 400ºF. In medium saucepan, heat olive oil over medium heat. Add onion, bell pepper, and carrots; cook and stir until crisp-tender, about 5 minutes. Add tomato paste, mustard, and water and bring to a simmer. Simmer, stirring frequently, for 5 minutes.
2. Spread the sauce over the pizza crust. Cut the meatballs in half and arrange on the pizza. Sprinkle with Cheddar and mozzarella cheeses.
3. Bake for 20–30 minutes or until crust is golden brown, pizza is hot, and cheese is melted and bubbling. Let stand for 5 minutes, then serve.

Nutrition Info:
- Info Per Serving: Calories:437.80; Fat: 15.85 g ;Saturated fat: 6.29g ;Sodium: 432.76 mg

Canadian-bacon Risotto

Servings: 6
Cooking Time: X

Ingredients:
- 2 cups water
- 3 cups Low-Sodium Chicken Broth
- 1 tablespoon olive oil
- 1 chopped onion
- 3 cloves garlic, minced
- 1 (8-ounce) package sliced mushrooms
- ½ teaspoon dried oregano leaves
- 1 teaspoon dried basil leaves
- 2 cups Arborio rice
- 1/8 teaspoon white pepper
- 1 cup chopped Canadian bacon
- ¼ cup shredded Parmesan cheese
- 1 tablespoon butter

Directions:
1. In medium saucepan, combine water and broth; heat over low heat until warm; keep on heat.
2. In large saucepan, heat olive oil over medium heat. Add onion, garlic, and mushrooms to pan; cook and stir until crisp-tender, about 4 minutes. Add oregano and basil.
3. Add rice; cook and stir for 2 minutes. Add the broth mixture, a cup at a time, stirring until the liquid is absorbed, about 15 minutes. When there is 1 cup broth remaining, add pepper and Canadian bacon along with the last cup of broth. Cook and stir until rice is tender, about 5 minutes.
4. Stir in Parmesan and butter and serve immediately.

Nutrition Info:
- Info Per Serving: Calories: 379.72; Fat: 9.41 g ;Saturated fat:3.17g ;Sodium: 292.55 mg

Pork Cutlets With Fennel And Kale

Servings: X
Cooking Time: 30 Minutes

Ingredients:
- 2 (4-ounce) boneless pork top-loin chops
- Sea salt
- Freshly ground black pepper
- 2 teaspoons olive oil, divided
- 1 small fennel bulb, thinly sliced
- ½ cup chopped sweet onion
- 1 teaspoon garlic
- ¼ cup white wine
- ¼ low-sodium chicken broth
- 2 cups shredded kale
- 2 teaspoons chopped fresh basil, for garnish

Directions:
1. Pound the pork chops to about ¼-inch thick between two sheets of parchment paper and season each with salt and pepper.
2. In a large skillet, heat 1 teaspoon olive oil over medium-high heat and sear the pork until lightly browned, about 4 minutes per side. Remove the pork and cover with foil to keep warm.
3. Add the remaining 1 teaspoon olive oil to the skillet and sauté the fennel, onions, and garlic until softened, 6 to 7 minutes.
4. Add the wine and chicken broth to the skillet and bring the liquid to a boil. Reduce the heat to low, then simmer until the liquid reduces by half, about 5 minutes.
5. Return the pork to the skillet and cook until the pork is tender, about 6 minutes.
6. Stir in the kale and simmer until the kale is wilted, about 4 more minutes.
7. Serve topped with basil.

Nutrition Info:
- Info Per Serving: Calories: 366 ; Fat: 20 g ;Saturated fat: 7 g ;Sodium: 264 mg

Poultry

Grilled Turkey And Veggie Kabobs

Servings: 4
Cooking Time: 10 Minutes

Ingredients:
- 1 pound turkey tenderloin
- Pinch salt
- ⅛ teaspoon cayenne pepper
- 1 yellow summer squash, cut into ½-inch slices
- 1 orange bell pepper, seeded and cut into 1-inch cubes
- 1 red bell pepper, seeded and cut into 1-inch cubes
- 3 scallions, cut into 2-inch pieces
- ¼ cup apple jelly
- 2 tablespoons fresh lemon juice
- 1 tablespoon butter
- 1 tablespoon low-sodium mustard
- 1 teaspoon dried oregano leaves

Directions:
1. Prepare and preheat the grill to medium heat.
2. Cut the turkey into 1-inch cubes, put on a plate, and sprinkle with the salt and cayenne pepper.
3. Thread the turkey cubes, alternating with the squash, orange bell pepper, red bell pepper, and scallion, onto kabob skewers.
4. In a small saucepan, combine the apple jelly, lemon juice, and butter. Heat over low heat until the apple jelly melts and the mixture is smooth, about 2 minutes. Stir in the mustard and oregano.
5. Place the kabobs on the hot grill and brush with some of the apple jelly mixture. Cover and grill for 4 minutes.
6. Uncover, turn the kabobs, and brush with more of the apple jelly mixture. Cover and grill for 3 minutes.
7. Uncover the grill and turn the kabobs, brushing with the remaining apple jelly mixture, and cook until the turkey registers 165°F on a meat thermometer, 2 to 3 minutes longer. Use all of the apple jelly mixture; if any is left, discard it.

Nutrition Info:
- Info Per Serving: Calories: 232 ; Fat : 5 g ;Saturated fat: 2 g ;Sodium: 194 mg

Tandoori Turkey Pizzas

Servings: 4
Cooking Time: 18 Minutes

Ingredients:
- 4 (6½-inch) whole-wheat pita breads
- 1 teaspoon olive oil
- 1 onion, chopped
- 4 cloves garlic, minced
- ½ pound ground turkey
- 1 (8-ounce) can no-salt-added tomato sauce
- 2 teaspoons curry powder
- ½ teaspoon smoked paprika
- ¼ teaspoon ground cumin
- ⅛ teaspoon cayenne pepper
- ¼ cup crumbled feta cheese
- 3 tablespoons low-fat plain Greek yogurt

Directions:
1. Preheat the oven to 425°F. Place the pita breads on a baking sheet lined with aluminum foil and set aside.
2. In a large skillet, heat the olive oil over medium heat. Add the onion and garlic and cook, stirring frequently, for 2 minutes.
3. Add the ground turkey and sauté, breaking up the meat. Cook for 5 minutes or until the turkey is no longer pink.
4. Add the tomato sauce, curry powder, paprika, cumin, and cayenne pepper to the sauce and bring to a simmer. Simmer over low heat for 1 minute.
5. Top the pita "pizzas" evenly with the turkey mixture. Sprinkle each with the feta cheese.
6. Bake for 10 to 12 minutes or until the pizzas are hot. Drizzle each pizza with the yogurt and serve immediately.

Nutrition Info:
- Info Per Serving: Calories: 308 ; Fat : 6 g ;Saturated fat: 2 g ;Sodium: 779 mg

Chicken Paillards With Mushrooms

Servings: 4
Cooking Time: X

Ingredients:
- 4 (3-ounce) chicken breasts
- 3 tablespoons flour
- 1/8 teaspoon salt
- 1/8 teaspoon cayenne pepper
- ½ teaspoon dried marjoram leaves
- 2 tablespoons olive oil
- 4 shallots, minced
- 1 cup sliced button mushrooms
- 1 cup sliced cremini mushrooms
- ½ cup Low-Sodium Chicken Broth
- ¼ cup dry white wine
- 1 teaspoon Worcestershire sauce
- 1 tablespoon cornstarch

Directions:
1. Place chicken breasts between two sheets of waxed paper and pound until ¼" thick. On shallow plate, combine flour, salt, pepper, and marjoram. Dredge chicken in flour mixture to coat.
2. In large skillet, heat olive oil over medium heat. Add chicken; sauté on first side for 3 minutes, then carefully turn and cook for 1 minute longer. Remove to platter and cover to keep warm.
3. Add shallots and mushrooms to skillet; cook and stir for 4–5 minutes until tender. Meanwhile, in small bowl combine broth, wine, Worcestershire sauce, and cornstarch, and mix well. Add to mushroom mixture and bring to a boil.
4. Return chicken to skillet; cook until chicken is hot and sauce bubbles and thickens. Serve immediately over brown rice, couscous, or pasta.

Nutrition Info:
- Info Per Serving: Calories:270.13; Fat:8.25g ;Saturated fat:1.71 g ;Sodium: 167.63 mg

Moroccan Chicken

Servings: 4
Cooking Time: 15 Minutes

Ingredients:
- 3 (4-ounce) boneless, skinless chicken thighs, cubed
- 1 teaspoon smoked paprika
- ½ teaspoon ground cinnamon
- ½ teaspoon ground cumin
- ⅛ teaspoon ground ginger
- 1 cup low-sodium chicken broth
- 2 tablespoons fresh lemon juice
- 1 tablespoon cornstarch
- 1 teaspoon olive oil
- 1 onion, chopped
- 3 cloves garlic, minced
- 2 cups sugar snap peas
- 1 cup shredded carrots

Directions:
1. Put the cubed chicken in a medium bowl. Sprinkle with the paprika, cinnamon, cumin, and ginger, and work the spices into the meat. Set aside.
2. In a small bowl, combine the chicken broth, lemon juice, and cornstarch and mix well. Set aside.
3. Heat the olive oil in a large nonstick skillet over medium-high heat. Add the chicken thighs, and sauté for 5 minutes or until the chicken starts to brown. Remove the chicken from the pan and set aside.
4. Add the onion and garlic to the skillet, and sauté for 3 minutes.
5. Add the sugar snap peas and carrots to the skillet and sauté for 2 minutes.
6. Return the chicken to the skillet and stir. Add the chicken broth mixture, bring to a simmer, and turn down the heat to low. Simmer 3 to 4 minutes or until the sauce thickens, the vegetables are tender, and the chicken is cooked to 165°F on a meat thermometer. Serve hot.

Nutrition Info:
- Info Per Serving: Calories: 165 ; Fat : 5 g ;Saturated fat: 1 g ;Sodium: 112 mg

Balsamic Blueberry Chicken

Servings: 2
Cooking Time: 25 Min

Ingredients:
- Aluminum foil
- ½ cup fresh blueberries
- 2 tbsp. pine nuts
- ¼ cup cilantro, chopped
- 2 tbsp. balsamic vinegar
- ¼ tsp ground black pepper
- 2 (4 oz) chicken breasts, butterflied

Directions:
1. Heat the olive oil in a medium-sized frying pan over medium Heat the oven to 375°F gas mark 5. Line a baking sheet with aluminum foil.
2. In a medium-sized mixing bowl, add the blueberries, pine nuts, cilantro, balsamic vinegar, and pepper, mix until well combined.
3. Place the chicken breasts on the baking sheet and pour the blueberry mixture on top.
4. Bake for 20 to 25 minutes, until the juices are caramelized, and the inside of the chicken has cooked through. Serve warm.

Nutrition Info:
- Info Per Serving: Calories: 212 ; Fat: 7 g ;Saturated fat:1 g ;Sodium: 58 mg

Piri Piri Chicken

Servings: 4
Cooking Time: 15 Minutes

Ingredients:
- 3 (6-ounce) boneless, skinless chicken breasts, cubed
- 2 tablespoons lemon juice
- 1 teaspoon smoked paprika
- ½ teaspoon cayenne pepper
- Pinch salt
- 2 teaspoons chili powder
- 1 teaspoon olive oil
- 1 onion, chopped
- 4 cloves garlic, minced
- 1 red bell pepper, chopped
- 1 red chile pepper, such as chile de arbol, seeded and minced
- 2 tablespoons Piri Piri sauce
- 1 cup low-sodium chicken broth
- 1 tablespoon cornstarch

Directions:
1. Place the chicken breasts in a medium bowl and drizzle with the lemon juice.
2. Sprinkle the chicken with the smoked paprika, cayenne pepper, salt, and chili powder. Work the spices into the chicken with your hands and set aside.
3. In a large nonstick skillet, heat the olive oil over medium heat.
4. Add the chicken to the skillet. Cook, stirring frequently, until the chicken is lightly browned, about 4 minutes. Transfer the chicken to a clean plate.
5. Add the onion, garlic, red bell pepper, red chile pepper, and Piri Piri sauce to the skillet stir. Sauté 3 to 4 minutes or until the vegetables are crisp-tender. Return the chicken to the skillet.
6. In a small bowl, combine the chicken broth and cornstarch and mix with a whisk. Stir into the chicken mixture.
7. Simmer 3 to 4 minutes or until the chicken is cooked to 165°F when tested with a meat thermometer, and the sauce is thickened. Serve immediately.

Nutrition Info:
- Info Per Serving: Calories: 209 ; Fat : 5 g ;Saturated fat: 1 g ;Sodium: 210 mg

Servings: 4
Cooking Time: 10 Minutes

Ingredients:
- 1 (8-ounce) can crushed pineapple, undrained
- ⅓ cup water
- 2 tablespoons cornstarch
- 1 teaspoon brown sugar
- 1 teaspoon low-sodium tamari sauce
- ¼ teaspoon ground ginger
- ⅛ teaspoon cayenne pepper
- 2 tablespoons unsweetened shredded coconut
- 2 tablespoons chopped macadamia nuts
- 2 teaspoons olive oil
- 1 onion, chopped
- 1 red bell pepper, seeded and chopped
- 3 (6-ounce) boneless, skinless chicken breasts, cubed

Directions:
1. In a medium bowl, combine the pineapple, water, cornstarch, brown sugar, tamari, ginger, and cayenne pepper, and mix well. Set aside.
2. Place a large nonstick skillet or wok over medium heat. Add the coconut and macadamia nuts, and toast for 1 to 2 minutes, stirring constantly, until fragrant. Remove from the skillet and set aside.
3. Add the olive oil to the skillet and heat over medium-high heat. Add the onion and red bell pepper, and stir-fry for 2 to 3 minutes or until almost tender.
4. Add the chicken to the wok, and stir-fry for 3 to 4 minutes or until lightly browned.
5. Stir the sauce, add to the skillet, and stir fry for 1 to 2 minutes longer until the sauce thickens and the chicken registers at 165°F when tested with a meat thermometer.
6. Serve immediately, topped with the toasted coconut and macadamia nuts.

Nutrition Info:
- Info Per Serving: Calories: 301 ; Fat : 12 g ;Saturated fat: 4 g ;Sodium: 131 mg

Turkey Curry With Fruit

Servings: 6
Cooking Time: X

Ingredients:
- 6 (4-ounce) turkey cutlets
- 1 tablespoon flour
- 1 tablespoon plus
- 1 teaspoon curry powder, divided
- 1 tablespoon olive oil
- 2 pears, chopped
- 1 apple, chopped ½ cup raisins
- 1 tablespoon sugar
- 1/8 teaspoon salt
- 1/3 cup apricot jam

Directions:
1. Preheat oven to 350°F. Spray a cookie sheet with sides with nonstick cooking spray. Arrange cutlets on prepared cookie sheet. In small bowl, combine flour, 1 tablespoon curry powder, and olive oil and mix well. Spread evenly over cutlets.
2. In medium bowl, combine pears, apple, raisins, sugar, salt, 1 teaspoon curry powder, and apricot jam, and mix well. Divide this mixture over the turkey cutlets.
3. Bake for 35–45 minutes or until turkey is thoroughly cooked and fruit is hot and caramelized. Serve immediately.

Nutrition Info:
- Info Per Serving: Calories: 371.52; Fat: 11.15 g ;Saturated fat: 2.80 g ;Sodium: 121.35 mg

Chicken Spicy Thai Style

Servings: 4
Cooking Time: X

Ingredients:
- 2 tablespoons lime juice
- 1 tablespoon low-sodium soy sauce
- ½ cup Low-Sodium Chicken Broth
- ¼ cup dry white wine
- ¼ cup natural peanut butter
- 2 tablespoons peanut oil
- 1 onion, chopped
- 4 cloves garlic, minced
- 3 (4-ounce) boneless, skinless chicken breasts, sliced
- 4 cups shredded Napa cabbage
- 1 cup shredded carrots

Directions:
1. In small bowl, combine lime juice, soy sauce, chicken broth, wine, and peanut butter and mix with wire whisk until blended. Set aside.
2. In wok or large skillet, heat peanut oil over medium-high heat. Add onion and garlic; stir-fry until crisp-tender, about 4 minutes. Add chicken; stir-fry until almost cooked, about 3 minutes. Add cabbage and carrots; stir-fry until cabbage begins to wilt, about 3–4 minutes longer.
3. Remove food from wok and return wok to heat. Add peanut butter mixture and bring to a simmer. Return chicken and vegetables to wok; stir fry until sauce bubbles and thickens and chicken is thoroughly cooked, about 3–4 minutes. Serve immediately.

Nutrition Info:
- Info Per Serving: Calories: 300.35; Fat:16.70 g ;Saturated fat:3.20 g;Sodium:309.32 mg

"butter" Chicken

Servings: 4
Cooking Time: 12 Minutes

Ingredients:
- 4 (6-ounce) boneless, skinless chicken breasts, cubed
- 2 tablespoons fresh lemon juice
- 2 teaspoons curry powder
- 1 teaspoon chili powder
- ⅛ teaspoon black pepper
- 2 teaspoons olive oil
- 1 onion, chopped
- 4 cloves garlic, minced
- ½ cup low-fat coconut milk
- ½ cup low-fat plain Greek yogurt
- 2 tablespoons no-salt-added tomato paste
- 1 tablespoon cornstarch

Directions:
1. In a large bowl, combine the chicken with the lemon juice, curry powder, chili powder, and black pepper, and mix with your hands, rubbing the spices into the chicken. Set aside.
2. In a large nonstick skillet, heat the olive oil over medium heat.
3. Add the onion and garlic, and sauté for 4 to 5 minutes, until tender.
4. Add the chicken and sauté, stirring frequently, until the chicken starts to brown, about 4 minutes.
5. Meanwhile, in a small bowl, combine the coconut milk, yogurt, tomato paste, and cornstarch, and mix well with a whisk.
6. Add the coconut milk mixture to the skillet. Simmer 4 to 5 minutes or until the sauce is thickened and the chicken registers 165°F on a meat thermometer. Serve hot.

Nutrition Info:
- Info Per Serving: Calories: 308 ; Fat : 8 g ;Saturated fat: 3 g ;Sodium: 144 mg

Chicken Breasts With Salsa

Servings: 4
Cooking Time: X

Ingredients:
- 2 tablespoons lime juice, divided
- 1 egg white
- 1 cup whole-grain cereal, crushed
- 1 teaspoon dried thyme leaves
- ¼ teaspoon pepper
- 4 (4-ounce) boneless, skinless chicken breasts
- 1 cup Super Spicy Salsa
- 1 jalapeño pepper, minced

Directions:
1. Preheat oven to 375ºF. Line a cookie sheet with a wire rack and set aside. In small bowl, combine 1 tablespoon lime juice and egg white; beat until frothy. On shallow plate, combine crushed cereal, thyme, and pepper.
2. Dip chicken into egg white mixture, then into cereal mixture to coat. Place on prepared cookie sheet. Bake for 20–25 minutes or until chicken is thoroughly cooked and coating is crisp.
3. Meanwhile, in small saucepan combine remaining 1 tablespoon lime juice, salsa, and jalapeño pepper. Heat through, stirring occasionally. Serve with chicken.

Nutrition Info:
- Info Per Serving: Calories: 264.05; Fat: 4.43 g ;Saturated fat:1.18 g ;Sodium: 146.85 mg

Asian Chicken Stir-fry

Servings: 4
Cooking Time: X

Ingredients:
- 2 (5-ounce) boneless, skinless chicken breasts
- ½ cup Low-Sodium Chicken Broth
- 1 tablespoon low-sodium soy sauce
- 1 tablespoon cornstarch
- 1 tablespoon sherry
- 2 tablespoons peanut oil
- 1 onion, sliced
- 3 cloves garlic, minced
- 1 tablespoon grated ginger root
- 1 cup snow peas
- ½ cup canned sliced water chestnuts, drained
- 1 yellow summer squash, sliced
- ¼ cup chopped unsalted peanuts

Directions:
1. Cut chicken into strips and set aside. In small bowl, combine chicken broth, soy sauce, cornstarch, and sherry and set aside.
2. In large skillet or wok, heat peanut oil over medium-high heat. Add chicken; stir-fry until almost cooked, about 3–4 minutes. Remove to plate. Add onion, garlic, and ginger root to skillet; stir-fry for 4 minutes longer. Then add snow peas, water chestnuts, and squash; stir-fry for 2 minutes longer.
3. Stir chicken broth mixture and add to skillet along with chicken. Stir-fry for 3–4 minutes longer or until chicken is thoroughly cooked and sauce is thickened and bubbly. Sprinkle with peanuts and serve immediately.

Nutrition Info:
- Info Per Serving: Calories: 252.42; Fat: 12.42 g ;Saturated fat:2.06 g ;Sodium: 202.04 mg

Cold Chicken With Cherry Tomato Sauce

Servings: 3
Cooking Time: X

Ingredients:
- 2 teaspoons fresh thyme leaves
- ½ cup Low-Sodium Chicken Broth
- 12 ounces boneless, skinless chicken breasts
- 1 tablespoon olive oil
- 3 cloves garlic, minced
- 2 cups cherry tomatoes
- ½ cup no-salt tomato juice
- ½ cup chopped fresh basil
- ¼ cup low-fat sour cream
- 1/8 teaspoon white pepper

Directions:
1. In large saucepan, combine thyme and chicken broth; bring to a simmer over medium heat. Add chicken and reduce heat to low. Cover and poach for 7–9 minutes or until chicken is thoroughly cooked.
2. Place chicken in a casserole dish just large enough to hold the chicken. Pour poaching liquid over, then cover and refrigerate for at least 8 hours.
3. When ready to eat, heat olive oil in large skillet. Add garlic; cook and stir for 1 minute. Then stir in cherry tomatoes; cook and stir until the tomatoes pop, about 4–6 minutes. Add tomato juice, basil, sour cream, and pepper; stir, and heat briefly.
4. Slice the chicken and fan out on serving plate. Top with tomato mixture and serve immediately.

Nutrition Info:
- Info Per Serving: Calories: 227.58; Fat: 8.63 g ;Saturated fat: 2.57 g ;Sodium: 198.32 mg

Italian Chicken Bake

Servings: 4
Cooking Time: 25 Min

Ingredients:
- 1 lb. chicken breasts, halved lengthwise into 4 pieces
- ½ tsp garlic powder
- ½ tsp fine sea salt
- ¼ tsp ground black pepper
- ¼ tsp Italian seasoning
- ½ cup basil, finely chopped
- 4 part-skim mozzarella cheese slices
- 2 large Roma tomatoes, finely chopped

Directions:
1. Heat the oven to 400°F gas mark 6.
2. Season the cut chicken breasts with garlic powder, salt, pepper and Italian seasoning.
3. Place the seasoned chicken breasts on a baking sheet. Bake for 18 to 22 minutes, or until the chicken breasts are cooked through. Remove from the oven and set it to broil on high.
4. Evenly place the basil, 1 mozzarella slice and tomatoes on each chicken breast.
5. Return the baking sheet to the oven and broil for 2 to 3 minutes, until the cheese has melted and browned.
6. Remove from the oven and serve hot.

Nutrition Info:
- Info Per Serving: Calories: 239 ; Fat: 9 g ;Saturated fat: 4 g ;Sodium: 524 mg

Chicken Breasts With New Potatoes

Servings: 6
Cooking Time: X

Ingredients:
- 12 small new red potatoes
- 2 tablespoons olive oil
- 1/8 teaspoon white pepper
- 4 cloves garlic, minced
- 1 teaspoon dried oregano leaves
- 2 tablespoons Dijon mustard
- 4 (4-ounce) boneless, skinless chicken breasts
- 1 cup cherry tomatoes

Directions:
1. Preheat oven to 400ºF. Line a roasting pan with parchment paper and set aside. Scrub potatoes and cut each in half. Place in prepared pan.
2. In small bowl, combine oil, pepper, garlic, oregano, and mustard and mix well. Drizzle half of this mixture over the potatoes and toss to coat. Roast for 20 minutes.
3. Cut chicken breasts into quarters. Remove pan from oven and add chicken to potato mixture. Using a spatula, mix potatoes and chicken together. Drizzle with remaining oil mixture. Return to oven and roast for 15 minutes longer.
4. Add tomatoes to pan. Roast for 5–10 minutes longer, or until potatoes are tender and browned and chicken is thoroughly cooked.

Nutrition Info:
- Info Per Serving: Calories: 395.92; Fat: 9.57 g ;Saturated fat: 1.85 g;Sodium: 142.98 mg

Pineapple Curried Chicken

Servings: 4
Cooking Time: 15 Minutes

Ingredients:
- 3 (6-ounce) boneless, skinless chicken breasts, cubed
- 2 teaspoons curry powder
- 2 tablespoons cornstarch
- ⅛ teaspoon cayenne pepper
- 1 teaspoon olive oil
- 2 shallots, minced
- 3 cloves garlic, minced
- 1 (16-ounce) can pineapple chunks, drained, reserving juice
- 2 teaspoons yellow curry paste (optional)
- ⅓ cup reserved pineapple juice
- 1 tablespoon fresh lemon juice
- 3 tablespoons plain nonfat Greek yogurt

Directions:
1. In a medium bowl, toss the chicken breast cubes with the curry powder, cornstarch, and cayenne pepper, and set aside.
2. In a large nonstick skillet, heat the olive oil over medium heat.
3. Add the shallots and garlic, and cook for 2 minutes, stirring frequently.
4. Add the coated chicken cubes. Cook and stir for 5 to 6 minutes or until the chicken starts to brown.
5. Add the pineapple chunks, yellow curry paste (if using), reserved pineapple juice, and lemon juice to the skillet and bring to a simmer.
6. Simmer for 3 to 4 minutes or until the chicken is cooked to 165°F when tested with a meat thermometer. Stir in the yogurt and serve hot.

Nutrition Info:
- Info Per Serving: Calories: 260 ; Fat : 3 g ;Saturated fat: 1 g ;Sodium: 93 mg

Chicken Rice

Servings: 2
Cooking Time: 25 Min

Ingredients:
- 1 cup brown basmati rice, cooked
- 1 cup chicken breast, cooked and chopped
- 1 cup spinach, cooked and shredded
- ½ cup low-sodium canned garbanzo beans, drained and rinsed
- 4 tbsp. lemon and herb vinaigrette, divided
- 1 large carrot, peeled and grated
- 1 large red bell pepper, diced
- 1 large green bell pepper, diced
- 1 cup frozen peas, cooked
- ½ cup frozen corn, cooked
- ¼ cup pine nuts, toasted for garnish

Directions:
1. In a medium-sized mixing bowl, add the basmati rice, chicken breasts, spinach, garbanzo beans and 2 tbsp. of the lemon and herb vinaigrette, mix to combine.
2. Divide the rice mixture between two large bowls and arrange the carrot, red bell pepper, green bell pepper, peas, and corn in the bowls and drizzle with the remaining lemon and herb vinaigrette.
3. Top with pine nuts and serve.

Nutrition Info:
- Info Per Serving: Calories: 503 ; Fat: 21 g ;Saturated fat:3 g ;Sodium: 187 mg

Lemon Tarragon Turkey Medallions

Servings: 4
Cooking Time: 10 Minutes

Ingredients:
- 1 pound turkey tenderloin
- Pinch salt
- ⅛ teaspoon lemon pepper
- 2 tablespoons cornstarch
- 1 teaspoon dried tarragon leaves
- ¼ cup fresh lemon juice
- ½ cup low-sodium chicken stock
- 1 teaspoon grated fresh lemon zest
- 2 teaspoons olive oil

Directions:
1. Cut the turkey tenderloin crosswise into ½-inch slices. Sprinkle with the salt and lemon pepper.
2. In a small bowl, combine the cornstarch, tarragon, lemon juice, chicken stock, and lemon zest, and mix well.
3. Heat the olive oil in a large nonstick skillet over medium heat.
4. Add the turkey tenderloins. Cook for 2 minutes, and then turn and cook for another 2 minutes.
5. Add the lemon juice mixture to the skillet. Cook, stirring frequently, until the sauce boils and thickens and the turkey is cooked to 165°F on a meat thermometer. Serve immediately.

Nutrition Info:
- Info Per Serving: Calories: 169 ; Fat :3 g ;Saturated fat: 1 g ;Sodium: 77 mg

Turkey With Prunes

Servings: 6
Cooking Time: X

Ingredients:
- 3 tablespoons olive oil
- 1 onion, chopped
- 3 cloves garlic, minced
- 1 cup finely chopped pitted prunes
- 1/8 teaspoon salt
- 1/8 teaspoon pepper
- ½ cup chopped hazelnuts
- 6 (3-ounce) turkey cutlets
- 2 tablespoons flour
- ½ cup Low-Sodium Chicken Broth
- ¼ cup dry white wine
- ½ teaspoon dried thyme leaves
- 1 tablespoon lemon juice

Directions:
1. In small saucepan, heat 1 tablespoon olive oil over medium heat. Add onion and garlic; cook and stir until crisp-tender, about 4 minutes. Add prunes and sprinkle with salt and pepper. Cook for 3–4 minutes or until prunes begin to plump. Add nuts and remove from heat. Let cool for 20 minutes.
2. Arrange turkey cutlets on work surface. Divide prune mixture among the cutlets. Roll up, securing with kitchen twine or toothpicks. Dredge filled cutlets in flour.
3. Heat remaining 2 tablespoons olive oil in large skillet. Brown turkey, turning to cook evenly, for about 4–5 minutes. Then add broth, wine, and thyme leaves to skillet. Cover and braise cutlets for 6–8 minutes or until turkey is tender and thoroughly cooked. Add lemon juice and serve immediately.

Nutrition Info:
- Info Per Serving: Calories: 327.80; Fat: 15.34 g ;Saturated fat: 2.04 g;Sodium: 92.23 mg

Crunchy Chicken Coleslaw Salad

Servings: 4
Cooking Time: 7 Minutes

Ingredients:
- 3 (6-ounce) boneless, skinless chicken breasts, cubed
- Pinch salt
- ⅛ teaspoon white pepper
- 1 teaspoon toasted sesame oil
- ¼ cup low-fat mayonnaise
- ¼ cup low-sodium chicken broth
- 2 tablespoons fresh lemon juice
- 1 tablespoon low-sodium yellow mustard
- 2 tablespoons chopped fresh dill
- 4 cups shredded red cabbage
- 1 small yellow summer squash, sliced
- 1 small carrot, shredded
- 2 tablespoons sunflower seeds

Directions:
1. Sprinkle the chicken with the salt and pepper.
2. Heat the sesame oil in a large nonstick skillet. Add the chicken and cook, stirring frequently, until lightly browned and cooked to 165°F when tested with a meat thermometer, about 5 to 7 minutes. Remove from the skillet and set aside.
3. In a large bowl, combine the mayonnaise, chicken broth, lemon juice, mustard, and dill and mix well.
4. Add the cabbage, squash, and carrot to the dressing in the bowl and toss.
5. Add the chicken to the salad and toss.
6. Sprinkle with the sunflower seeds and serve.

Nutrition Info:
- Info Per Serving: Calories: 256; Fat : 9 g ;Saturated fat: 2 g ;Sodium: 169 mg

Chicken Pesto

Servings: 6
Cooking Time: X

Ingredients:
- 1 cup packed fresh basil leaves
- ¼ cup toasted chopped hazelnuts
- 2 cloves garlic, chopped
- 2 tablespoons olive oil
- 1 tablespoons water
- ¼ cup grated Parmesan cheese
- ½ cup Low-Sodium Chicken Broth
- 12 ounces boneless, skinless chicken breasts
- 1 (12-ounce) package angel hair pasta

Directions:
1. Bring a large pot of salted water to a boil. In blender or food processor, combine basil, hazelnuts, and garlic. Blend or process until very finely chopped. Add olive oil and water; blend until a paste forms. Then blend in Parmesan cheese; set aside.
2. In large skillet, bring chicken broth to a simmer over medium heat. Cut chicken into strips and add to broth. Cook for 4 minutes, then add the pasta to the boiling water.
3. Cook pasta for 3–4 minutes according to package directions, until al dente. Drain and add to chicken mixture; cook and stir for 1 minute until chicken is thoroughly cooked. Add basil mixture, remove from heat, and stir until a sauce forms. Serve immediately.

Nutrition Info:
- Info Per Serving: Calories: 373.68; Fat: 11.06 g ;Saturated fat: 2.01 g ;Sodium: 108.92 mg

Hot-and-spicy Peanut Thighs

Servings: 4
Cooking Time: X

Ingredients:
- 4 (4-ounce) chicken thighs
- ½ cup low-sodium barbecue sauce
- 2 teaspoons chili powder
- ½ cup chopped unsalted peanuts

Directions:
1. Preheat oven to 350ºF. Spray a roasting pan with nonstick cooking spray and set aside. Pound chicken slightly, to " thickness.
2. In shallow bowl, combine barbecue sauce and chili powder and mix well. Dip chicken into sauce, then dip one side into peanuts. Place, peanut side up, in prepared pan.
3. Bake for 30–40 minutes, or until chicken is thoroughly cooked and nuts are browned. Serve immediately.

Nutrition Info:
- Info Per Serving: Calories: 327.41; Fat: 19.55 g ;Saturated fat: 4.22 g;Sodium: 129.88 mg

Turkey Cutlets Parmesan

Servings: 6
Cooking Time: X

Ingredients:
- 1 egg white
- ¼ cup dry breadcrumbs
- 1/8 teaspoon pepper
- 4 tablespoons grated Parmesan cheese, divided
- 6 (4-ounce) turkey cutlets
- 2 tablespoons olive oil
- 1 (15-ounce) can no-salt tomato sauce
- 1 teaspoon dried Italian seasoning
- ½ cup finely shredded part-skim mozzarella cheese

Directions:
1. Preheat oven to 350ºF. Spray a 2-quart baking dish with nonstick cooking spray and set aside.
2. In shallow bowl, beat egg white until foamy. On plate, combine breadcrumbs, pepper, and 2 tablespoons Parmesan. Dip the turkey cutlets into the egg white, then into the breadcrumb mixture, turning to coat.
3. In large saucepan, heat olive oil over medium heat. Add turkey cutlets; brown on both sides, about 2–3 minutes per side. Place in prepared baking dish. Add tomato sauce and Italian seasoning to saucepan; bring to a boil.
4. Pour sauce over cutlets in baking pan and top with mozzarella cheese and remaining 2 tablespoons Parmesan. Bake for 25–35 minutes or until sauce bubbles and cheese melts and begins to brown. Serve with pasta, if desired.

Nutrition Info:
- Info Per Serving: Calories: 275.49; Fat: 10.98 g ;Saturated fat:3.43 g ;Sodium: 229.86 mg

Turkey Cutlets Florentine

Servings: 6
Cooking Time: X

Ingredients:
- 1 egg white, beaten
- ½ cup dry breadcrumbs
- 1/8 teaspoon white pepper
- 2 tablespoons grated Parmesan cheese
- 6 (4-ounce) turkey cutlets
- 2 tablespoons olive oil
- 2 cloves minced garlic
- 2 (8-ounce) bags fresh baby spinach
- 1/8 teaspoon ground nutmeg
- 1/3 cup shredded Jarlsberg cheese

Directions:
1. In shallow bowl, place egg white and beat until foamy. On shallow plate, combine breadcrumbs, pepper, and Parmesan and mix well.
2. Place turkey cutlets between waxed paper and pound to " thickness if necessary. Dip cutlets into egg white, then into breadcrumb mixture to coat.
3. In large saucepan, heat olive oil over medium-high heat. Add turkey; cook for 4 minutes. Carefully turn and cook for 4–6 minutes longer, until thoroughly cooked. Remove to serving plate and cover with foil to keep warm.
4. Add garlic to drippings remaining in pan; cook and stir for 1 minute. Then add spinach and nutmeg; cook and stir until spinach wilts, about 4–5 minutes. Add the Jarlsberg, top with the turkey, cover, and remove from heat. Let stand for 2 minutes to melt cheese, then serve.

Nutrition Info:
- Info Per Serving: Calories: 258.57; Fat:9.19 g ;Saturated fat:2.15 g ;Sodium: 236.98mg

Mediterranean Patties

Servings: 4
Cooking Time: 15 Min

Ingredients:
- Aluminium foil
- 1 cup broccoli florets
- 1 small red onion, quartered
- ¼ cup black olives, pitted
- 8 oz baby spinach, roughly chopped
- 1 lb. ground chicken
- 1½ tsp Mediterranean Seasoning Rub Blend
- 4 whole wheat buns
- Lettuce
- Tomato

Directions:
1. Preheat the oven to broil. Line a baking sheet with aluminum foil.
2. In a food processor, pulse the broccoli, onion, and olives for 1 to 2 minutes, until minced.
3. In a large-sized mixing bowl, add the baby spinach, broccoli mixture, chicken, and the Mediterranean spice blend, mix to combine. Form into 8 medium-sized patties and place them on the baking sheet.
4. Broil for 10 minutes on one side, flip, then broil for 3 minutes on the other side until golden brown.
5. Serve on wholewheat buns with lettuce and tomato, or with a garden salad.

Nutrition Info:
- Info Per Serving: Calories: 206 ; Fat: 10 g ;Saturated fat: 3 g ;Sodium: 134 mg

Fish And Seafood

Fish And Seafood

Fried Mahi-mahi

Servings: 4
Cooking Time: 20 Min

Ingredients:
- 1 lb. mahi-mahi fillets
- ½ tsp fine sea salt
- ¼ tsp ground black pepper
- 1 tbsp. olive oil
- 1 medium green bell pepper, cored and chopped
- 1 small brown onion, chopped
- 2 cups grape tomatoes
- ¼ cup black olives, pitted and chopped

Directions:
1. Season the mahi-mahi fillets with salt and pepper.
2. Heat the olive oil in a large nonstick frying pan over medium-high heat.
3. Add the green bell pepper and onion. Cook for 3 to 5 minutes, until softened.
4. Add the grape tomatoes and black olives. Mix for 1 to 2 minutes, until the tomatoes have softened.
5. Place the mahi-mahi fillets on top of the vegetables and cover with a lid. Cook for 5 to 10 minutes, or until the fish flakes with a fork. Remove from the heat and serve.

Nutrition Info:
- Info Per Serving: Calories: 151 ; Fat: 5 g ;Saturated fat: 1 g ;Sodium: 603 mg

Flounder Fillet Bake

Servings: 4
Cooking Time: 15 Min

Ingredients:
- Aluminum foil
- 4 (4 oz) flounder fillets
- 2 tbsp. avocado oil
- 1 tsp ground thyme
- ½ tsp Himalayan pink salt
- ¼ tsp ground black pepper
- 1 lime, cut into wedges
- 2 tbsp. cilantro, finely chopped

Directions:
1. Heat the oven to 400°F gas mark 6. Line a baking sheet with aluminum foil.
2. Place the flounder fillets on the baking sheet and drizzle with avocado oil.
3. Season both sides of the fillets with thyme, salt pepper.
4. Bake for 6 to 8 minutes, flip, and bake for a further 5 minutes, or until cooked through. Remove from the oven.
5. Serve the flounder fillets with a lime wedge and sprinkle with cilantro.

Nutrition Info:
- Info Per Serving: Calories: 164 ; Fat: 8 g ;Saturated fat: 1 g ;Sodium: 369 mg

Red Snapper Scampi

Servings: 4
Cooking Time: 20 Minutes

Ingredients:
- 2 teaspoons olive oil
- 4 cloves garlic, minced
- ¼ cup fresh lemon juice
- ¼ cup white wine or fish stock
- 1 teaspoon fresh lemon zest
- Pinch salt
- ⅛ teaspoon lemon pepper
- 4 (6-ounce) red snapper fillets
- 2 scallions, minced
- 3 tablespoons minced flat-leaf fresh parsley

Directions:
1. Preheat the oven to 400°F. Line a baking pan with parchment paper.
2. In a small bowl, combine the olive oil, garlic, lemon juice, white wine, lemon zest, salt, and lemon pepper.
3. Arrange the fillets skin side down, if the skin is attached, on the prepared baking pan. Pour the lemon juice mixture over the fillets.
4. Roast for 15 to 20 minutes, or until the fish flakes when tested with a fork.
5. Serve the fish with the pan drippings, sprinkled with the scallions and parsley.

Nutrition Info:
- Info Per Serving: Calories: 212 ; Fat: 5 g ;Saturated fat: 1 g;Sodium: 112 mg

Salmon With Spicy Mixed Beans

Servings: 4
Cooking Time: 20 Minutes

Ingredients:
- 2 teaspoons olive oil, divided
- 4 (4-ounce) salmon fillets
- Pinch salt
- ⅛ teaspoon black pepper
- 1 onion, diced
- 3 cloves peeled garlic, minced
- 1 jalapeño pepper, seeded and minced
- 1 (16-ounce) can low-sodium mixed beans, rinsed and drained
- 2 tablespoons low-fat plain Greek yogurt
- 2 tablespoons minced fresh cilantro

Directions:
1. Put 1 teaspoon of the olive oil in a large skillet and heat over medium heat.
2. Sprinkle the salmon fillets with the salt and pepper and add to the skillet, skin side down.
3. Cook for 5 minutes, then flip the fillets with a spatula and cook for another 3 to 4 minutes or until the salmon flakes when tested with a fork. Remove the fish to a clean warm plate, and cover with an aluminum foil tent to keep warm.
4. Add the remaining 1 teaspoon of the olive oil to the skillet. Add the onion, garlic, and jalapeño pepper; cook, stirring frequently, for 3 minutes.
5. Add the beans and mash with a fork until desired consistency.
6. Remove the pan from the heat, add the yogurt, and stir until combined.
7. Pile the beans onto a serving platter, top with the fish, and sprinkle with the cilantro. Serve immediately.

Nutrition Info:
- Info Per Serving: Calories: 293 ; Fat: 10 g ;Saturated fat: 2 g;Sodium: 345 mg

Seafood Risotto

Servings: 6
Cooking Time: X

Ingredients:
- 2 cups water
- 2½ cups Low-Sodium Chicken Broth
- 2 tablespoons olive oil
- 1 onion, minced
- 3 cloves garlic, minced
- 1½ cups Arborio rice
- 1 cup chopped celery
- 1 tablespoon fresh dill weed
- ¼ cup dry white wine
- ½ pound sole fillets
- ¼ pound small raw shrimp
- ½ pound bay scallops
- ¼ cup grated Parmesan cheese
- 1 tablespoon butter

Directions:
1. In medium saucepan, combine water and broth and heat over low heat. Keep mixture on heat.
2. In large saucepan, heat olive oil over medium heat. Add onion and garlic; cook and stir until crisp-tender, about 3 minutes. Add rice; cook and stir for 3 minutes.
3. Start adding broth mixture, a cup at a time, stirring frequently, adding liquid when previous addition is absorbed. When only 1 cup of broth remains to be added, stir in celery, dill, wine, fish fillets, shrimp, and scallops to rice mixture. Add last cup of broth.
4. Cook, stirring constantly, for 5–7 minutes or until fish is cooked and rice is tender and creamy. Stir in Parmesan and butter, stir, and serve.

Nutrition Info:
- Info Per Serving: Calories:397.22 ; Fat:11.11 g ;Saturated fat:3.20 g ;Sodium:354.58 mg

Grilled Scallops With Gremolata

Servings: 4
Cooking Time: 6 Minutes

Ingredients:
- 2 scallions, cut into pieces
- ¾ cup packed fresh flat-leaf parsley
- ¼ cup packed fresh basil leaves
- 1 teaspoon lemon zest
- 3 tablespoons fresh lemon juice
- 1 tablespoon olive oil
- 20 sea scallops
- 2 teaspoons butter, melted
- Pinch salt
- ⅛ teaspoon lemon pepper

Directions:
1. Prepare and preheat the grill to medium-high. Make sure the grill rack is clean.
2. Meanwhile, make the gremolata. In a blender or food processor, combine the scallions, parsley, basil, lemon zest, lemon juice, and olive oil. Blend or process until the herbs are finely chopped. Pour into a small bowl and set aside.
3. Put the scallops on a plate. If the scallops have a small tough muscle attached to them, remove and discard it. Brush the melted butter over the scallops. Sprinkle with the salt and the lemon pepper.
4. Place the scallops in a grill basket, if you have one. If not, place a sheet of heavy-duty foil on the grill, punch some holes in it, and arrange the scallops evenly across it.
5. Grill the scallops for 2 to 3 minutes per side, turning once, until opaque. Drizzle with the gremolata and serve.

Nutrition Info:
- Info Per Serving: Calories: 190 ; Fat: 7 g ;Saturated fat: 2 g;Sodium: 336 mg

Halibut Parcels

Servings: 4
Cooking Time: 15 Min

Ingredients:
- Aluminum foil
- 4 cups kale, stems removed and shredded
- 2 cups button mushrooms, sliced
- 4 (4 oz) halibut fillets
- ½ tsp seafood seasoning
- ½ tsp fine sea salt
- ¼ tsp ground black pepper
- ¼ cup spring onion, chopped
- 2 tbsp. olive oil

Directions:
1. Heat the oven to 425°F gas mark 7.
2. Prepare the aluminum foil by tearing them into squares, big enough for the fillets and vegetables.
3. Place 1 cup of kale and ½ cup of mushroom onto each foil square.
4. Place the halibut fillet on top of each parcel. Season with seafood seasoning, salt and pepper.
5. Sprinkle the spring onion over this and drizzle with olive oil.
6. Fold the foil to seal in the halibut and vegetables.
7. Place on a baking sheet and bake for 15 minutes. Remove from the oven and carefully unfold the parcels.

Nutrition Info:
- Info Per Serving: Calories:155 ; Fat: 7 g ;Saturated fat: 1 g ;Sodium: 435 mg

Red Snapper With Fruit Salsa

Servings: 4
Cooking Time: X

Ingredients:
- 1 cup blueberries
- 1 cup chopped watermelon
- 1 jalapeño pepper, minced
- ½ cup chopped tomatoes
- 3 tablespoons olive oil, divided
- 2 tablespoons orange juice
- 1/8 teaspoon salt, divided
- 1/8 teaspoon white pepper
- 4 (4-ounce) red snapper fillets
- 1 lemon, thinly sliced

Directions:
1. Preheat oven to 400ºF. Spray a 9″ glass baking pan with nonstick cooking spray and set aside. In medium bowl, combine blueberries, watermelon, jalapeño pepper, tomatoes, 1 tablespoon olive oil, orange juice, and half of the salt. Mix well and set aside.
2. Arrange fillets in prepared pan. Sprinkle with remaining salt and the white pepper and drizzle with 2 tablespoons olive oil. Top with lemon slices.
3. Bake for 15 to 20 minutes, or until fish is opaque and flesh flakes when tested with fork. Place on serving plate and top with blueberry mixture; serve immediately.

Nutrition Info:
- Info Per Serving: Calories: 254.40; Fat:12.01 g ;Saturated fat:1.82 g ;Sodium:186.42 mg

Broiled Swordfish

Servings: 4
Cooking Time: X

Ingredients:
- 1 tablespoon olive oil
- 2 tablespoons dry white wine
- 1 teaspoon lemon zest
- ¼ teaspoon salt
- 1/8 teaspoon white pepper
- 1 teaspoon dried dill weed
- 1¼ pounds swordfish steaks
- 4 ½-inch-thick tomato slices

Directions:
1. Preheat broiler. In small bowl, combine oil, wine, zest, salt, pepper, and dill weed and whisk to blend.
2. Place steaks on broiler pan. Brush steaks with oil mixture. Broil 6″ from heat for 4 minutes. Turn fish and brush with remaining oil mixture. Top with tomatoes. Return to broiler and broil for 4–6 minutes or until fish flakes when tested with fork.

Nutrition Info:
- Info Per Serving: Calories: 210.97 ; Fat:9.10 g ;Saturated fat: 2.03 g ;Sodium:273.91 mg

Citrus-blueberry Fish En Papillote

Servings: 4
Cooking Time: X

Ingredients:
- 1 tablespoon olive oil
- 1 onion, finely chopped
- 4 cloves garlic, minced
- 2 tablespoons lemon juice
- 2 tablespoons orange juice
- 1 teaspoon orange zest
- 4 (4-ounce) sole or mahi mahi fillets
- 1 cup blueberries
- 2 tablespoons blueberry jam

Directions:
1. Preheat oven to 400°F. Cut parchment paper into four large heart shapes measuring about 12″ × 18″. Fold hearts in half, open up, then set aside.
2. In small saucepan, heat olive oil over medium heat. Add onion and garlic; cook and stir for 4 minutes until crisp-tender. Remove from heat and stir in lemon and orange juice along with orange zest.
3. Place one fillet at the center of each parchment heart, next to the fold. Divide onion mixture among fillets. In small bowl, combine blueberries and blueberry jam and mix gently. Divide on top of onion mixture.
4. Fold one half of the parchment heart over the other. Crimp and fold the edges to seal. Place on cookie sheets. Bake for 18–23 minutes or until the bundles are puffed and the paper is browned.
5. Serve immediately, warning diners to be careful of the steam that will billow out when the packages are opened.

Nutrition Info:
- Info Per Serving: Calories:220.81 ; Fat:5.18 g ;Saturated fat:0.87 g ;Sodium:116.46 mg

Salmon With Farro Pilaf

Servings: 4
Cooking Time: 25 Minutes

Ingredients:
- ½ cup farro
- 1¼ cups low-sodium vegetable broth
- 4 (4-ounce) salmon fillets
- Pinch salt
- ½ teaspoon dried marjoram leaves
- ⅛ teaspoon white pepper
- ¼ cup dried cherries
- ¼ cup dried currants
- 1 cup fresh baby spinach leaves
- 1 tablespoon orange juice

Directions:
1. Preheat the oven to 400°F. Line a baking sheet with parchment paper and set aside.
2. In a medium saucepan over medium heat, combine the farro and the vegetable broth and bring to a simmer. Reduce the heat to low and simmer, partially covered, for 25 minutes, or until the farro is tender.
3. Meanwhile, sprinkle the salmon with the salt, marjoram, and white pepper and place on the prepared baking sheet.
4. When the farro has cooked for 10 minutes, bake the salmon in the oven for 12 to 15 minutes, or until the salmon flakes when tested with a fork. Remove and cover to keep warm.
5. When the farro is tender, add the cherries, currants, spinach, and orange juice; stir and cover. Let stand off the heat for 2 to 3 minutes.
6. Plate the salmon and serve with the farro pilaf.

Nutrition Info:
- Info Per Serving: Calories: 304 ; Fat: 8 g ;Saturated fat: 2 g;Sodium: 139 mg

Servings: 6
Cooking Time: X

Ingredients:
- 1 egg white
- ¼ cup dry breadcrumbs
- 1/3 cup ground almonds
- 1/8 teaspoon salt
- 1/8 teaspoon white pepper
- 6 (4-ounce) red snapper fillets
- 3 tablespoons olive oil, divided
- 1 onion, chopped
- 4 cloves garlic, minced
- 1 red bell pepper, chopped
- ¼ pound small raw shrimp
- 1 tablespoon lemon juice
- ½ cup low-fat sour cream
- ½ teaspoon dried dill weed

Directions:
1. Place egg white in shallow bowl; beat until foamy. On shallow plate, combine breadcrumbs, almonds, salt, and pepper and mix well. Dip fish into egg white, then into crumb mixture, pressing to coat. Let stand on wire rack for 10 minutes.
2. In small saucepan, heat 1 tablespoon olive oil over medium heat. Add onion, garlic, and bell pepper; cook and stir until tender, about 5 minutes. Add shrimp; cook and stir just until shrimp curl and turn pink, about 1–2 minutes. Remove from heat and add lemon juice; set aside.
3. In large saucepan, heat remaining 2 tablespoons olive oil over medium heat. Add coated fish fillets. Cook for 4 minutes on one side, then carefully turn and cook for 2–5 minutes on second side until coating is browned and fish flakes when tested with a fork.
4. While fish is cooking, return saucepan with shrimp to medium heat. Add sour cream and dill weed. Heat, stirring, until mixture is hot.
5. Remove fish from skillet and place on serving plate. Top each with a spoonful of shrimp sauce and serve immediately.

Nutrition Info:
- Info Per Serving: Calories:272.57 ; Fat:13.80 g ;Saturated fat: 3.09 g;Sodium:216.17 mg

Scallops On Skewers With Tomatoes

Servings: 4
Cooking Time: X

Ingredients:
- 1 pound sea scallops
- 12 cherry tomatoes
- 4 green onions, cut in half crosswise
- ½ cup chopped parsley
- 1 tablespoon fresh oregano leaves
- 3 tablespoons olive oil
- 2 tablespoons lemon juice
- 2 cloves garlic
- 1/8 teaspoon salt
- 1/8 teaspoon pepper

Directions:
1. Prepare and preheat broiler. Rinse scallops and pat dry. Thread on skewers along with cherry tomatoes and green onions.
2. In blender or food processor, combine remaining ingredients. Blend or process until smooth. Reserve ¼ cup of this sauce.
3. Brush remaining sauce onto the food on the skewers. Place on broiler pan. Broil 6″ from heat for 3–4 minutes per side, turning once during cooking time. Serve with remaining sauce.

Nutrition Info:
- Info Per Serving: Calories:202.03 ; Fat:11.11 g ;Saturated fat: 1.52 g ;Sodium:251.50 mg

Salmon With Mustard And Orange

Servings: 4
Cooking Time: X

Ingredients:
- 4 (5-ounce) salmon fillets
- 1 tablespoon olive oil
- 2 tablespoons Dijon mustard
- 1 tablespoon flour
- 1 teaspoon orange zest
- 2 tablespoons orange juice Pinch salt
- 1/8 teaspoon white pepper

Directions:
1. Preheat broiler. Place fillets on a broiler pan. In small bowl, combine remaining ingredients and mix well. Spread over salmon.
2. Broil fish 6″ from heat for 7–10 minutes or until fish flakes when tested with fork and topping bubbles and begins to brown. Serve immediately.

Nutrition Info:
- Info Per Serving: Calories: 277.64; Fat:14.02 g ;Saturated fat:2.09 g ;Sodium:197.84 mg

Cod Satay

Servings: 4
Cooking Time: 15 Minutes

Ingredients:
- 2 teaspoons olive oil, divided
- 1 small onion, diced
- 2 cloves garlic, minced
- ⅓ cup low-fat coconut milk
- 1 tomato, chopped
- 2 tablespoons low-fat peanut butter
- 1 tablespoon packed brown sugar
- ⅓ cup low-sodium vegetable broth
- 2 teaspoons low-sodium soy sauce
- ⅛ teaspoon ground ginger
- Pinch red pepper flakes
- 4 (6-ounce) cod fillets
- ⅛ teaspoon white pepper

Directions:
1. In a small saucepan, heat 1 teaspoon of the olive oil over medium heat.
2. Add the onion and garlic, and cook, stirring frequently for 3 minutes.
3. Add the coconut milk, tomato, peanut butter, brown sugar, broth, soy sauce, ginger, and red pepper flakes, and bring to a simmer, stirring with a whisk until the sauce combines. Simmer for 2 minutes, then remove the satay sauce from the heat and set aside.
4. Season the cod with the white pepper.
5. Heat a large nonstick skillet with the remaining 1 teaspoon olive oil, and add the cod fillets. Cook for 3 minutes, then turn and cook for 3 to 4 minutes more or until the fish flakes when tested with a fork.
6. Cover the fish with the satay sauce and serve immediately.

Nutrition Info:
- Info Per Serving: Calories: 255 ; Fat: 10 g ;Saturated fat: 5 g;Sodium: 222 mg

Scallops On Skewers With Lemon

Servings: 4
Cooking Time: X

Ingredients:
- 2 tablespoons lemon juice
- 1 teaspoon grated lemon zest
- 2 teaspoons sesame oil
- 2 tablespoons chili sauce
- 1/8 teaspoon cayenne pepper
- 1 pound sea scallops
- 4 strips low-sodium bacon

Directions:
1. Prepare and preheat grill or broiler. In medium bowl, combine lemon juice, zest, sesame oil, chili sauce, and cayenne pepper and mix well. Add scallops and toss to coat. Let stand for 15 minutes.
2. Make skewers with the scallops and bacon. Thread a skewer through one end of the bacon, then add a scallop. Curve the bacon around the scallop and thread onto the skewer so it surrounds the scallop halfway. Repeat with 3 to 4 more scallops and the bacon slice.
3. Repeat with remaining scallops and bacon. Grill or broil 6″ from heat source for 3–5 minutes per side, until bacon is crisp and scallops are cooked and opaque. Serve immediately.

Nutrition Info:
- Info Per Serving: Calories:173.65 ; Fat:6.48 g ;Saturated fat: 1.51 g;Sodium:266.64 mg

Halibut Burgers

Servings: 4
Cooking Time: 35 Min

Ingredients:
- Aluminum foil
- 1 lb. halibut fillets
- ½ tsp Himalayan pink salt, divided
- ¼ tsp ground black pepper
- ½ cup whole wheat breadcrumbs
- 1 large free-range egg
- 1 tbsp. garlic, crushed
- ½ tsp dried dill
- 2 tbsp. avocado oil
- 4 whole wheat buns

Directions:
1. Heat the oven to 400°F gas mark 6. Line a baking sheet with aluminum foil.
2. Place the halibut fillets on the baking sheet and season with ¼ tsp salt and pepper. Bake for 15 to 20 minutes, or until the halibut flakes with a fork. Remove from the oven.
3. Transfer the flesh into a medium-sized mixing bowl, removing any bones.
4. Add the breadcrumbs, egg, garlic, dill and the remaining ¼ tsp salt, mix to combine.
5. Mold the fish mixture into 4 patties.
6. Heat the avocado oil in a large heavy bottom pan over medium heat.
7. Gently place the halibut patties in the pan. Fry for 5 to 6 minutes, until browned, flip, and cook for 3 to 5 minutes, remove from the heat.
8. Place 1 fish patty on each of the 4 buns and serve.

Nutrition Info:
- Info Per Serving: Calories: 294 ; Fat: 16 g ;Saturated fat: 3 g ;Sodium: 458 mg

Seared Scallops With Fruit

Servings: 3–4
Cooking Time: X

Ingredients:
- 1 pound sea scallops Pinch salt
- 1/8 teaspoon white pepper
- 1 tablespoon olive oil
- 1 tablespoon butter or margarine
- ¼ cup dry white wine
- 2 peaches, sliced
- 1 cup blueberries
- 1 tablespoon lime juice

Directions:
1. Rinse scallops and pat dry. Sprinkle with salt and pepper and set aside.
2. In large skillet, heat olive oil and butter over medium-high heat. Add the scallops and don't move them for 3 minutes. Carefully check to see if the scallops are deep golden brown. If they are, turn and cook for 1–2 minutes on the second side.
3. Remove scallops to serving plate. Add peaches to skillet and brown quickly on one side, about 2 minutes. Turn peaches and add wine to skillet; bring to a boil. Remove from heat and add blueberries. Pour over scallops, sprinkle with lime juice, and serve immediately.

Nutrition Info:
- Info Per Serving: Calories: 207.89; Fat: 7.36 g ;Saturated fat:2.40 g ;Sodium: 242.16 mg

Tuna Patties

Servings: 6
Cooking Time: 10 Min

Ingredients:
- 12 oz canned, water-packed tuna, drained
- 4 tbsp. almond flour
- 1 large free-range egg white
- 1 tbsp. brown onion, finely chopped
- ½ lemon, juiced
- ½ tsp parsley, finely chopped
- Pinch red pepper flakes
- Pinch Himalayan pink salt
- Pinch ground black pepper
- Cooking spray

Directions:
1. In a medium-sized mixing bowl, add the tuna, almond flour, egg white, onions, lemon juice, parsley, red pepper flakes, salt, and pepper, mix to combine.
2. Mold the tuna mixture into 6 equal patties.
3. Place the tuna cakes on a plate and chill for 1 hour in the refrigerator until firm.
4. Spray a large, heavy-bottom pan with cooking spray and place it over medium-high heat.
5. Add the tuna cakes to the pan and cook for 5 minutes per side, turning once, until browned and heated through. Serve.

Nutrition Info:
- Info Per Serving: Calories: 243 ; Fat: 6 g ;Saturated fat: 0 g ;Sodium: 558 mg

Northwest Salmon

Servings: 4
Cooking Time: X

Ingredients:
- 4 tablespoons olive oil, divided
- 5 juniper berries, crushed
- ½ cup chopped red onion
- 1 cup blueberries
- ½ cup chopped hazelnuts
- ¼ cup dry white wine
- 4 (5-ounce) salmon fillets Pinch salt
- 1/8 teaspoon white pepper
- 2 cups watercress

Directions:
1. Preheat grill or broiler. In small saucepan, heat 3 tablespoons of the olive oil. Add juniper berries and red onion; cook and stir for 3 minutes. Add blueberries, hazelnuts, and wine and bring to a simmer.
2. Meanwhile, sprinkle salmon with salt and pepper and brush with olive oil. Broil or grill 6″ from heat until salmon flakes when tested with a fork. Place salmon on watercress and pour blueberry sauce over all; serve immediately.

Nutrition Info:
- Info Per Serving: Calories: 362.66; Fat:22.63 g ;Saturated fat:3.27 g ;Sodium: 105.81 mg

Fennel-grilled Haddock

Servings: 4
Cooking Time: X

Ingredients:
- 2 bulbs fennel
- 4 (5-ounce) haddock or halibut steaks
- 3 tablespoons olive oil Pinch salt
- 1/8 teaspoon cayenne pepper
- 1 teaspoon paprika
- 2 tablespoons lemon juice

Directions:
1. Prepare and preheat grill. Slice fennel bulbs lengthwise into ½" slices, leaving the stalks and fronds attached.
2. Brush fennel and haddock with olive oil on all sides to coat. Sprinkle fish with salt, pepper, and paprika. Place fennel on grill 6″ above medium coals, cut side down. Arrange fish on top of fennel and close the grill.
3. Grill for 5–7 minutes or until fennel is deep golden brown and fish flakes when tested with fork. Remove fish to serving platter, sprinkle with lemon juice, and cover.
4. Cut the root end and stems from the fennel and discard. Slice fennel and place on top of fish; serve immediately.

Nutrition Info:
- Info Per Serving: Calories: 246.68; Fat: 11.35 g ;Saturated fat:1.58 g ;Sodium: 192.31 mg

Poached Chilean Sea Bass With Pears

Servings: 4
Cooking Time: X

Ingredients:
- ½ cup dry white wine
- ¼ cup water
- 2 bay leaves
- 1/8 teaspoon salt
- ½ teaspoon Tabasco sauce
- 1 lemon, thinly sliced
- 4 (4–5) ounce sea bass steaks or fillets
- 2 firm pears, cored and cut in half
- 1 tablespoon butter

Directions:
1. In large skillet, combine wine, water, bay leaves, salt, Tabasco, and lemon slices. Bring to a simmer over medium heat.
2. Add fish and pears. Reduce heat to low and poach for 9–12 minutes or until fish flakes when tested with a fork.
3. Remove fish and pears to serving platter. Remove bay leaves from poaching liquid and increase heat to high. Boil for 3–5 minutes or until liquid is reduced and syrupy. Swirl in butter and pour over fish and pears; serve immediately.

Nutrition Info:
- Info Per Serving: Calories:235.38 ; Fat: 5.81 g ;Saturated fat: 2.55 g ;Sodium:194.06 mg

Mediterranean Roasted Mahi Mahi With Broccoli

Servings: 4
Cooking Time: 22 Minutes

Ingredients:
- 2 cups broccoli florets
- 2 tablespoons olive oil, divided
- 4 (6-ounce) mahi mahi fillets
- 1 cup cherry tomatoes
- 2 cloves peeled garlic, sliced
- ⅛ teaspoon white pepper
- 1 teaspoon paprika
- 2 tablespoons fresh lemon juice
- 2 tablespoons crumbled feta cheese

Directions:
1. Preheat the oven to 400°F. Line a baking sheet with parchment paper.
2. Place the broccoli florets on the prepared baking sheet. Drizzle with 1 tablespoon of the olive oil and toss to coat. Spread the broccoli in a single layer.
3. Roast the broccoli for 10 minutes.
4. Remove the baking sheet from the oven. Move the broccoli over to make room for the fish. Place the fish, cherry tomatoes, and garlic on the baking sheet. Sprinkle the fish with the white pepper and paprika.
5. In a small bowl, combine the lemon juice and the remaining 1 tablespoon olive oil, and drizzle over the fish and vegetable mixture.
6. Roast for 10 to 12 minutes longer, or until the fish flakes when tested with a fork and the broccoli is tender.
7. Sprinkle with the feta cheese and serve immediately.

Nutrition Info:
- Info Per Serving: Calories: 258; Fat: 11 g ;Saturated fat: 2 g;Sodium: 171 mg

Shrimp And Pineapple Lettuce Wraps

Servings: 4
Cooking Time: 12 Minutes

Ingredients:
- 2 teaspoons olive oil
- 2 jalapeño peppers, seeded and minced
- 6 scallions, chopped
- 2 yellow bell peppers, seeded and chopped
- 8 ounces small shrimp, peeled and deveined
- 2 cups canned pineapple chunks, drained, reserving juice
- 2 tablespoons fresh lime juice
- 1 avocado, peeled, and cubed
- 1 large carrot, coarsely grated
- 8 romaine or Boston lettuce leaves, rinsed and dried

Directions:
1. In a medium saucepan, heat the olive oil over medium heat.
2. Add the jalapeño pepper and scallions and cook for 2 minutes, stirring constantly.
3. Add the bell pepper, and cook for 2 minutes.
4. Add the shrimp, and cook for 1 minute, stirring constantly.
5. Add the pineapple, 2 tablespoons of the reserved pineapple juice, and lime juice, and bring to a simmer. Simmer for 1 minute longer or until the shrimp curl and turn pink. Let the mixture cool for 5 minutes.
6. Serve the shrimp mixture with the cubed avocado and grated carrot, wrapped in the lettuce leaves.

Nutrition Info:
- Info Per Serving: Calories: 241 ; Fat: 9 g ;Saturated fat: 2 g;Sodium: 109 mg

Servings: 2
Cooking Time: 15 Min

Ingredients:
- 12 oz zucchini spirals
- 2 tsp low-sodium tamari sauce
- 2 tsp apple cider vinegar
- 1 tsp ginger, peeled and grated
- 1 tsp garlic, crushed
- 1 tsp organic honey
- 2 tsp sesame oil
- 6 oz shrimp, peeled and deveined
- 2 cups napa cabbage, shredded
- 1 medium green bell pepper, thinly sliced
- 1 spring onion, thinly sliced
- 1 tbsp. toasted sesame seeds, for garnish

Directions:
1. Cook the zucchini according to the package directions. Drain and run under cold water to stop the cooking process. Transfer the zucchini to a medium-sized mixing bowl and set aside.
2. In a small-sized mixing bowl, add the tamari sauce, apple cider vinegar, ginger, garlic, and honey, mix to combine, and set aside.
3. Warm the sesame oil in a medium-sized, heavy-bottom pan over medium-high heat. Add the shrimp and fry for 5 minutes until cooked through.
4. Add the napa cabbage, green bell pepper, and spring onion and fry for 4 minutes until the vegetables are tender. Add the tamari sauce mixture and the zucchini, toss to coat, heat for 1 minute.
5. Serve into bowls and top with sesame seeds.

Nutrition Info:
- Info Per Serving: Calories: 400 ; Fat: 8 g ;Saturated fat: 1 g ;Sodium: 347 mg

Soups, Salads, And Sides

Tangy Fish And Tofu Soup

Servings: 5
Cooking Time: 10 Minutes

Ingredients:
- 1 pound white fish (such as tilapia), thinly sliced
- ⅓ cup Tangy Soy Sauce
- 8 cups water
- 4 cups chopped napa cabbage
- 1 white onion, chopped
- 12 ounces soft tofu, cubed

Directions:
1. Place the fish and the Tangy Soy Sauce in a resealable plastic bag. Place the bag in the refrigerator and let the fish marinate for 30 minutes.
2. Once marinated, bring the water to a boil in a large pot over high heat. Add the cabbage and onion and bring to a boil again.
3. Add the tofu, marinated fish, and any remaining marinade to the pot.
4. Bring the soup back to a boil, reduce the heat to medium, and simmer for 5 minutes, until fragrant. Serve immediately.

Nutrition Info:
- Info Per Serving: Calories :181 ; Fat: 4g ;Saturated fat: 1g ;Sodium: 271 mg

Citrus Sparagus

Servings: 2
Cooking Time: 5 Min

Ingredients:
- ½ tsp olive oil
- ½ cup walnuts, finely chopped
- ½ lime, juiced and zested
- Himalayan pink salt
- Ground black pepper
- ½ lb. asparagus, woody ends trimmed

Directions:
1. Warm the olive oil in a small-sized, nonstick frying pan, over medium heat.
2. Add the walnuts and fry for 4 minutes until fragrant and golden brown.
3. Remove the pan from the heat and mix in the lime zest and juice.
4. Season the walnut mixture with salt and pepper to taste, set aside.
5. Fill a medium-sized stockpot with water and bring to the boil over high heat.
6. Blanch the asparagus for 2 minutes until al dente.
7. Discard the water and arrange the asparagus on a serving plate.
8. Sprinkle the walnut topping over the vegetables and serve.

Nutrition Info:
- Info Per Serving: Calories: 192 ; Fat:15 g ;Saturated fat: 1 g ;Sodium: 10 mg

Summer Pineapple Fruit Salad

Servings: 8
Cooking Time: X

Ingredients:
- 1 cup lemon yogurt
- ¼ cup nonfat whipped salad dressing
- 1 teaspoon lemon zest
- 2 tablespoons honey
- 1 teaspoon chopped fresh thyme
- 1 fresh pineapple
- 1 cantaloupe
- 1 honeydew melon
- 2 cups sliced strawberries
- 1 pint blueberries
- 1 cup raspberries

Directions:
1. In large bowl, combine yogurt, salad dressing, lemon zest, and honey, and mix well. Stir in thyme and set aside.
2. Twist top off pineapple and discard. Slice pineapple in half, then cut off rind. Cut into quarters, then cut out center core. Slice pineapple and add to yogurt mixture.
3. Cut cantaloupe and melon in half, scoop out seeds and discard, and peel. Cut into cubes and add to yogurt mixture along with strawberries and blueberries. Toss gently and top with raspberries. Serve immediately, or cover and refrigerate up to 4 hours.

Nutrition Info:
- Info Per Serving: Calories:201.31; Fat:3.63 g ;Saturated fat:0.73 g;Sodium: 94.22 mg

Broccoli Slaw

Servings: 2
Cooking Time: 25 Min

Ingredients:
- For the dressing:
- 3 tbsp. organic apple cider vinegar
- 2 tbsp. avocado oil
- 1 tbsp. organic honey
- 1 tsp thyme, chopped
- Pinch red pepper flakes, (optional)
- Himalayan pink salt
- Ground black pepper
- For the salad:
- 2 cups broccoli slaw
- 2 carrots, peeled and grated
- 1 medium red bell pepper, julienned
- 1 medium yellow bell pepper, julienned
- 2 cups baby spinach, shredded
- 2 tbsp. golden raisins
- 2 tbsp. sliced almonds

Directions:
1. To make the dressing:
2. In a small Pyrex jug, add the apple cider vinegar, avocado oil, honey, and thyme, whisk until well blended.
3. Season with salt and pepper and set aside.
4. To make the salad:
5. In a medium-sized mixing bowl, add the broccoli slaw, carrots, red and yellow bell peppers, baby spinach, golden raisins, and almonds, drizzle with the dressing and toss until combined.
6. Serve cold.

Nutrition Info:
- Info Per Serving: Calories: 358 ; Fat: 18g;Saturated fat: 2g ;Sodium: 84 mg

Watermelon, Edamame, And Radish Salad

Servings: X
Cooking Time: X

Ingredients:
- 4 cups diced watermelon
- 2 cups shelled edamame
- 4 radishes, quartered
- 2 cups kale, torn into bite-size pieces
- ¼ cup Lemon-Cilantro Vinaigrette or store-bought balsamic vinaigrette
- ½ cup crumbled fat-free feta cheese, for garnish
- ¼ cup roasted, unsalted pumpkin seeds, for garnish

Directions:
1. In a medium bowl, add the watermelon, edamame, radishes, and kale.
2. Add the dressing and toss to coat.
3. Serve topped with feta and pumpkin seeds.

Nutrition Info:
- Info Per Serving: Calories: 514 ; Fat: 24 g ;Saturated fat: 3 g ;Sodium: 400 mg

Fresh Creamy Fruit Dip

Servings: 6
Cooking Time: X

Ingredients:
- 1 (3-ounce) package light cream cheese, softened
- 1 cup vanilla yogurt
- 2 tablespoons honey
- 2 tablespoons orange juice
- 2 tablespoons brown sugar

Directions:
1. In medium bowl, beat cream cheese until light and fluffy. Gradually add yogurt, beating until smooth. Add honey, orange juice, and brown sugar and beat well. Cover and chill for at least 4 hours before serving.

Nutrition Info:
- Info Per Serving: Calories: 99.31; Fat:3.14g ;Saturated fat:1.98 g ;Sodium: 72.66 mg

Creamy Garlic Hummus

Servings: 6–8
Cooking Time: X

Ingredients:
- 1 head Roasted Garlic
- 1 (15-ounce) can no-salt garbanzo beans
- ½ cup Yogurt Cheese
- 2 tablespoons lemon juice
- ¼ cup tahini
- 2 tablespoons olive oil
- 3 tablespoons toasted sesame seeds

Directions:
1. Remove garlic from the papery skins and place in blender or food processor. Rinse and drain garbanzo beans and add to blender along with Yogurt Cheese, lemon juice, and tahini.
2. Blend or process until smooth. Place in serving bowl and drizzle with olive oil. Sprinkle with sesame seeds and serve with Seeded Breadsticks , pita chips, and crackers.

Nutrition Info:
- Info Per Serving: Calories:231.54; Fat: 11.71 g ;Saturated fat: 1.57 g ;Sodium: 26.76 mg

Apple Coleslaw

Servings: 6
Cooking Time: X

Ingredients:
- 1 cup plain yogurt
- ¼ cup low-fat mayonnaise
- ¼ cup buttermilk
- 2 tablespoons mustard
- 2 tablespoons lemon juice
- 1 tablespoon chopped fresh tarragon leaves
- 2 Granny Smith apples, chopped
- 3 cups shredded red cabbage
- 3 cups shredded green cabbage
- ½ cup walnut pieces, toasted

Directions:
1. In large bowl, combine yogurt, mayonnaise, buttermilk, mustard, lemon juice, and tarragon leaves; mix well to blend. Add chopped apples, red cabbage, and green cabbage and mix well.
2. Cover and chill in refrigerator for 2–4 hours before serving. Sprinkle with walnuts before serving.

Nutrition Info:
- Info Per Serving: Calories: 184.33; Fat:10.59 g ;Saturated fat:1.36 g;Sodium: 188.36 mg

Barbeque Tofu Salad

Servings: 2
Cooking Time: 5 Min

Ingredients:
- 1 tsp olive oil
- ¼ cup medium red onion, diced
- ½ tbsp. garlic, minced
- 4 oz tofu, crumbled
- 2 tsp unsalted tomato paste
- ¼ cup water
- ¼ tsp barbeque dry rub
- 1 head iceberg lettuce, roughly chopped
- 1 cup Roma tomatoes, diced
- 1 medium cucumber, quartered and sliced
- ¼ ripe avocado, peeled, pitted, and sliced
- 2 tbsp. Chile lime dressing

Directions:
1. Heat the olive oil in a medium-sized, heavy-bottom pan over medium-low heat. Add the onion and garlic. Fry for 1 minute, until the onion becomes translucent.
2. Add the tofu, tomato paste, water, and barbeque dry rub, stirring constantly for 3 minutes until lightly browned.
3. Divide the iceberg lettuce, tomatoes, cucumber, tofu mixture, and avocado slices into two serving bowls. Drizzle the salad with Chile lime dressing. Serve cold.

Nutrition Info:
- Info Per Serving: Calories:225 ; Fat:11g ;Saturated fat: 1g ;Sodium:11 mg

Banana To Go

Servings: 1
Cooking Time: 5 Min

Ingredients:
- 2 tbsp. cashew butter
- 2 tbsp. raisins
- 1 whole-wheat tortilla
- 1 banana

Directions:
1. Spread the cashew butter on the whole-wheat tortilla and sprinkle with raisins.
2. Place the banana in the middle of the tortilla with the cashew butter and wrap it up. Cut in half if you like or enjoy as is.

Nutrition Info:
- Info Per Serving: Calories: 433 ; Fat:22 g ;Saturated fat: 4g ;Sodium: 361 mg

Indian Vegetable Soup

Servings: 2-4
Cooking Time: 25 Min

Ingredients:
- 1 tsp coconut oil
- ½ cup red onion, finely chopped
- 1 tsp garlic, crushed
- 1 tsp ginger, peeled and grated
- 1 small cauliflower head, roughly chopped
- 1 cup canned lentils, rinsed and drained
- 4 cups low-sodium vegetable broth
- 1 tbsp. mild curry powder
- Himalayan pink salt
- ¼ cup low-fat plain yoghurt
- 1 tsp parsley, chopped for garnish

Directions:
1. Heat the coconut oil in a large stockpot over medium-high heat.
2. Add the onion, garlic, and ginger, fry for 3 minutes until softened.
3. Mix in the cauliflower, lentils, vegetable broth, and curry powder, allow the mixture to boil.
4. Reduce the heat to low and simmer for 20 minutes until the cauliflower is tender.
5. Transfer the soup to a food processor and process until no lumps remain.
6. Pour the soup back into the stockpot and mix in the plain yoghurt.
7. Garnish with chopped parsley and serve hot.

Nutrition Info:
- Info Per Serving: Calories: 231 ; Fat: 3 g ;Saturated fat: 0 g ;Sodium: 141 mg

Savory Chicken And Watermelon Rind Soup

Servings: 4
Cooking Time: 35 Minutes

Ingredients:
- 1 tablespoon olive oil
- ¾ pound boneless, skinless chicken thighs
- 2 tablespoons minced garlic
- 1 teaspoon peeled minced fresh ginger
- Pinch sea salt
- Pinch freshly ground black pepper
- 6 cups water
- 3 cups diced watermelon rind

Directions:
1. In a large stockpot, heat the olive oil over medium heat. Add the chicken, garlic, ginger, salt, and pepper, and sauté until the chicken is no longer pink, about 5 minutes.
2. Add the water to the pot, increase the heat to high, and bring the soup to a boil.
3. Add the watermelon rind once the water comes to a boil.
4. Allow the soup to come to a boil again, reduce the heat to medium, and simmer for 30 minutes.
5. Add more salt, if desired, and enjoy immediately.

Nutrition Info:
- Info Per Serving: Calories: 157 ; Fat: 7 g ;Saturated fat: 1g ;Sodium: 121 mg

Hearty Bean And Quinoa Stew

Servings: 4
Cooking Time: 20 Minutes

Ingredients:
- ½ tablespoon olive oil
- 1½ tablespoons minced garlic
- 1 cup diced carrots
- Pinch sea salt
- Pinch freshly ground black pepper
- 3 cups water
- ½ cup dry quinoa
- 1 (27-ounce) can no-salt-added diced tomatoes
- 1 (18-ounce) can no-salt-added red kidney beans, drained and rinsed

Directions:
1. In a medium pot, heat the olive oil over high heat. Add the garlic, carrots, salt, and pepper and sauté for 3 minutes, until fragrant.
2. To the same pot, add the water, quinoa, tomatoes with their juices, and beans. Increase the heat to high and bring to a boil.
3. Once the mixture comes to a boil, lower the heat to medium and simmer until the quinoa is soft, about 15 minutes. Serve immediately.

Nutrition Info:
- Info Per Serving: Calories: 248 ; Fat: 3g ;Saturated fat: 1g ;Sodium: 188 mg

Fennel-and-orange Salad

Servings: 4
Cooking Time: X

Ingredients:
- 2 fresh oranges
- 1 fennel bulb
- 4 scallions, trimmed and finely chopped
- 3 tablespoons olive oil
- 1 teaspoon fennel seeds, crushed
- 2 tablespoons lemon juice
- 1 tablespoon mustard
- 1/8 teaspoon white pepper
- 1 jalapeño pepper, minced, if desired
- 4 cups baby spinach leaves
- ¼ cup sliced almonds, toasted

Directions:
1. Peel the oranges, and slice them thinly crosswise. Set aside. Trim the fennel and remove the outer layer. Using a mandoline or vegetable peeler, shave the fennel into thin ribbons.
2. In small bowl, combine scallions, oil, fennel seeds, lemon juice, mustard, pepper, and jalapeño, if using. Whisk thoroughly until combined.
3. Arrange spinach leaves on chilled salad plates. Top with the orange slices and fennel. Drizzle with dressing, sprinkle with almonds, and serve immediately.

Nutrition Info:
- Info Per Serving: Calories:193.25 ; Fat:13.54 g ;Saturated fat:1.66 g ;Sodium: 148.69 mg

Tangy Mint Salad

Servings: 2
Cooking Time: 10 Min

Ingredients:
- 2 tbsp. avocado oil
- 2 tsp apple cider vinegar
- ¼ cup mint leaves, chopped
- 6 medium red radishes, cut into rounds
- 1 large English cucumber, cut into rounds
- 1 (8 oz) bag rocket
- Ground black pepper

Directions:
1. In a large-sized mixing bowl, add the avocado oil, apple cider vinegar, and mint, mix to combine.
2. Add the radishes, cucumber, and rocket, mix until everything is well incorporated. Season with pepper and serve immediately.

Nutrition Info:
- Info Per Serving: Calories: 140 ; Fat:14 g ;Saturated fat: 2g ;Sodium: 9 mg

Corn And Tomato Bean Salad

Servings: 5
Cooking Time: 15 Minutes

Ingredients:
- 1 (18-ounce) can low-sodium black beans, drained and rinsed
- 1 (12-ounce) can low-sodium corn, drained
- 1 cup diced tomato
- ¼ cup fresh minced cilantro
- 1 cup Fresh Lime Salsa

Directions:
1. In a medium bowl, combine the black beans, corn, tomato, cilantro, and the Fresh Lime Salsa. Enjoy immediately.

Nutrition Info:
- Info Per Serving: Calories: 181 ; Fat: 1 g ;Saturated fat: 0 g ;Sodium: 218 mg

Balsamic Vinaigrette

Servings: 9
Cooking Time: X

Ingredients:
- 2/3 cup extra-virgin olive oil
- 1/3 cup aged balsamic vinegar
- 1 teaspoon Worcestershire sauce
- 2 cloves garlic, minced
- 1 tablespoon lemon juice
- 1 tablespoon honey
- ¼ teaspoon salt
- 1/8 teaspoon white pepper

Directions:
1. Whisk all ingredients together. Cover and store in refrigerator for up to 3 days. Drizzle over salad greens or use as called for in recipes.

Nutrition Info:
- Info Per Serving: Calories:151.96; Fat: 16.00 g ;Saturated fat:2.21 g;Sodium: 71.49 mg

Caramelized Spiced Carrots

Servings: 6
Cooking Time: X

Ingredients:
- 1¼ pounds baby carrots
- ¼ cup orange juice
- 1/8 teaspoon salt
- 1/8 teaspoon white pepper
- 1 teaspoon grated orange zest
- 1 tablespoon sugar
- 1 tablespoon grated ginger root
- 1 tablespoon butter or plant sterol margarine

Directions:
1. In large saucepan, combine carrots, orange juice, salt, and pepper. Bring to a boil over high heat, then reduce heat to low, cover, and cook for 3–4 minutes or until carrots are crisp-tender.
2. Add orange zest, sugar, ginger root, and butter and bring to a boil over high heat. Cook until most of the orange juice evaporates and the carrots start to brown, stirring frequently, about 4–5 minutes. Serve immediately.

Nutrition Info:
- Info Per Serving: Calories: 62.66 ; Fat: 2.07 g ;Saturated fat: 1.24 g ;Sodium: 135.88 mg

Winter Noodle Soup

Servings: 4
Cooking Time: 45 Min

Ingredients:
- 1 tsp olive oil
- 1 (16 oz) package frozen spinach
- 1 cup leeks (stems included), cut into bite-size pieces
- 2 cups coriander, chopped
- 1½ cups cilantro, chopped
- 1½ cups water
- 1½ cups canned low-sodium garbanzo beans, drained and rinsed
- 1½ cups canned low-sodium black beans, drained and rinsed
- ¼ cup brown lentils
- ½ tsp ground turmeric
- ½ tsp ground black pepper
- ⅛ box of whole wheat spaghetti
- 2 tbsp. whole wheat flour, as needed

Directions:
1. In a large-sized stockpot, heat the olive oil over medium heat. Add the spinach and leek pieces, fry for 3 minutes, until the spinach has defrosted, and the leeks are translucent.
2. Add the coriander, cilantro, water, garbanzo beans, black beans, brown lentils, turmeric, and pepper. Bring to a boil and then simmer on medium-low heat for 30 minutes.
3. Add the whole-wheat spaghetti, making sure the noodles are covered by the liquid. Cook for 10 minutes.
4. If any water remains, add the flour as needed until it becomes slightly thickened. Serve hot.

Nutrition Info:
- Info Per Serving: Calories: 338; Fat: 5 g ;Saturated fat: 1 g ;Sodium: 116 mg

Black Bean Soup

Servings: 5
Cooking Time: 25 Minutes

Ingredients:
- 1 tablespoon olive oil
- 1 cup chopped carrots
- 1 white onion, chopped
- 1 tablespoon minced garlic
- Pinch sea salt
- Pinch freshly ground black pepper
- 4 cups water
- 2 (19-ounce) cans low-sodium black beans, drained and rinsed
- ⅓ cup fresh cilantro, chopped

Directions:
1. In a large stockpot, heat the olive oil over high heat. Add the carrots, onion, garlic, salt, and pepper and cook for 3 minutes until fragrant.
2. Add the water and black beans and bring the soup to a boil. Reduce the heat to medium and simmer until the beans are soft, about 20 minutes.
3. Working in batches, carefully transfer the soup to a blender (or use a handheld immersion blender) and blend until smooth.
4. Top with cilantro and serve immediately.

Nutrition Info:
- Info Per Serving: Calories: 182; Fat: 3g ;Saturated fat: 1g ;Sodium: 51 mg

Low-sodium Beef Broth

Servings: 10
Cooking Time: X

Ingredients:
- 3 pounds soup bones
- 1 pound beef shank
- 4 carrots, cut into
- 1"chunks
- 2 onions, chopped
- 2 tablespoons olive oil
- 2 bay leaves
- 5 cloves garlic, crushed
- 5 peppercorns
- 8 cups water

Directions:
1. Preheat oven to 400ºF. In large roasting pan, place soup bones, beef shank, carrots, and onions. Drizzle with olive oil and toss to coat. Roast for 2 hours or until bones and vegetables are brown.
2. Place roasted bones and vegetables along with bay leaves, garlic, and peppercorns in a 5- to 6-quart slow cooker. Pour 1 cup water into roasting pan and scrape up brown bits; add to slow cooker. Then pour remaining water into slow cooker. Cover and cook on low for 8–9 hours.
3. Strain broth into large bowl; discard solids. Cover broth and refrigerate overnight. In the morning, remove fat solidified on surface and discard. Pour broth into freezer containers, seal, label, and freeze up to 3 months. To use, defrost in refrigerator over-night.

Nutrition Info:
- Info Per Serving: Calories:31.45 ; Fat:0.88g ;Saturated fat: 0.29 g;Sodium: 15.65 mg

Stuffed Jalapeño Peppers

Servings: 6
Cooking Time: X

Ingredients:
- 12 small jalapeños
- 1 (3-ounce) package low-fat cream cheese, softened
- 1 tablespoon lemon juice
- ¼ cup Super Spicy Salsa
- 1 teaspoon chopped fresh oregano

Directions:
1. Cut jalapeños in half lengthwise. For a milder taste, remove membranes and seeds. Set aside.
2. In small bowl, combine cream cheese with lemon juice; beat until fluffy. Add salsa and oregano and mix well.
3. Using a small spoon, fill each jalapeño half with the cream cheese mixture. Serve immediately or cover and chill for up to 8 hours before serving.

Nutrition Info:
- Info Per Serving: Calories: 45.98; Fat:2.70 g ;Saturated fat:1.60 g ;Sodium:51.15 mg

Scalloped Potatoes With Aromatic Vegetables

Servings: 8
Cooking Time: X

Ingredients:
- 2 carrots, peeled and sliced
- 2 parsnips, peeled and sliced
- 3 russet potatoes, sliced
- ¼ cup olive oil
- 1/8 teaspoon salt
- 1/8 teaspoon white pepper
- 1 onion, finely chopped
- 4 cloves garlic, minced
- 1/3 cup grated Parmesan cheese
- ¼ cup dry breadcrumbs
- 1 cup milk

Directions:
1. Preheat oven to 375°F. Spray a 9″ × 13″ baking dish with nonstick cooking spray and set aside.
2. In large bowl, combine carrots, parsnips, and potatoes; drizzle with olive oil, sprinkle with salt and pepper, and toss to coat. Layer vegetables in prepared baking dish, sprinkling each layer with onion, garlic, Parmesan, and breadcrumbs, finishing with breadcrumbs.
3. Pour milk into casserole. Cover tightly with foil. Bake for 45 minutes, then uncover. Bake for 15–25 minutes longer or until vegetables are tender and top is browned. Serve immediately.

Nutrition Info:
- Info Per Serving: Calories:271.60 ; Fat:9.04 g ;Saturated fat: 2.03 g;Sodium: 211.64 mg

Salmon Pâté

Servings: 8
Cooking Time: X

Ingredients:
- 1 (14-ounce) can no-salt-added red sockeye salmon
- 1 (8-ounce) package nonfat cream cheese, softened
- ½ cup finely minced red onion
- ½ cup low-fat mayonnaise
- 1 tablespoon fresh dill weed, minced
- 2 tablespoons lime juice
- ½ teaspoon Tabasco sauce
- 1/8 teaspoon white pepper

Directions:
1. Drain salmon well; remove skin and bones, if desired. Combine all ingredients in blender or food processor. Blend or process until mixture is smooth.
2. Spoon into serving bowl, cover, and chill for 2–3 hours before serving.

Nutrition Info:
- Info Per Serving: Calories:167.26; Fat: 9.07g ;Saturated fat: 1.83g ;Sodium: 301.51 mg

Greek Quesadillas

Servings: 8
Cooking Time: X

Ingredients:
- 1 cucumber
- 1 cup plain yogurt
- ½ teaspoon dried oregano leaves
- 1 tablespoon lemon juice
- ½ cup crumbled feta cheese
- 4 green onions, chopped
- 3 plum tomatoes, chopped
- 1 cup fresh baby spinach leaves
- 1 cup shredded part-skim mozzarella cheese
- 12 (6-inch) no-salt corn tortillas

Directions:
1. Peel cucumber, remove seeds, and chop. In small bowl, combine cucumber with yogurt, oregano, and lemon juice and set aside.
2. In medium bowl, combine feta cheese, green onions, tomatoes, baby spinach, and mozzarella cheese and mix well.
3. Preheat griddle or skillet. Place six tortillas on work surface. Divide tomato mixture among them. Top with remaining tortillas and press down gently.
4. Cook quesadillas, pressing down occasionally with spatula, until tortillas are lightly browned. Flip quesadillas and cook on second side until tortillas are crisp and cheese is melted. Cut quesadillas in quarters and serve with yogurt mixture.

Nutrition Info:
- Info Per Serving: Calories:181.26 ; Fat: 6.34 g ;Saturated fat:3.62 g ;Sodium: 208.14 mg

Vegetarian Mains

Ratatouille

Servings: 6
Cooking Time: X

Ingredients:
- 3 tablespoons olive oil
- 2 onions, chopped
- 4 cloves garlic, minced
- 1 green bell pepper, sliced
- 1 yellow bell pepper, sliced
- 1 eggplant, peeled and cubed
- ¼ teaspoon salt
- 1/8 teaspoon pepper
- 2 tablespoons flour
- 2 zucchini, sliced
- 1 tablespoon red-wine vinegar
- 2 tablespoons capers, rinsed
- ¼ cup chopped flat-leaf parsley

Directions:
1. In large saucepan, heat olive oil over medium heat. Add onion and garlic; cook and stir until crisp-tender, about 3 minutes. Add bell peppers; cook and stir until crisp-tender, about 3 minutes.
2. Sprinkle eggplant with salt, pepper, and flour. Add to saucepan; cook and stir until eggplant begins to soften. Add remaining ingredients except parsley; cover, and simmer for 30–35 minutes or until vegetables are soft and mixture is blended. Sprinkle with parsley and serve.

Nutrition Info:
- Info Per Serving: Calories:124.26; Fat:7.10 g ;Saturated fat:1.02 g ;Sodium: 187.22 mg

Garbanzo Sandwich

Servings: 4
Cooking Time: 10 Min

Ingredients:
- 1 (15 oz) can low-sodium garbanzo bean, drained and rinsed
- ¼ cup medium red onion, finely chopped
- ¼ cup plain unsweetened coconut milk yoghurt
- 1½ tsp whole-grain mustard
- Himalayan pink salt
- Ground black pepper
- 2 green leaf lettuce leaves
- 4 whole-grain bread slices

Directions:
1. In a medium-sized mixing bowl, use a fork to mash up the garbanzo beans roughly. There must be some chunky pieces.
2. Add the red onion, coconut milk yoghurt, and wholegrain mustard. Season with salt and pepper to taste, mix to combine.
3. Place 1 green leaf lettuce leaf on each of the 2 wholegrain bread slices. Divide the garbanzo bean mixture between the 2 slices of bread on top of the lettuce leaf.
4. Top with the remaining slice of bread and serve.

Nutrition Info:
- Info Per Serving: Calories: 162; Fat: 3 g ;Saturated fat: 1 g ;Sodium: 287mg

Bean And Veggie Cassoulet

Servings: X
Cooking Time: 25 Minutes

Ingredients:
- 1 teaspoon olive oil
- ½ cup chopped sweet onion
- ½ cup chopped celery
- ½ cup shredded carrot
- 1 teaspoon minced garlic
- 1 cup low-sodium canned pinto beans, rinsed and drained
- 1 cup low-sodium canned black beans, rinsed and drained
- 1 cup low-sodium canned lentils, rinsed and drained
- 1 cup low-sodium vegetable broth
- 2 large tomatoes, chopped
- 1 cup shredded Swiss chard or collard greens
- 1 teaspoon chopped fresh oregano
- ½ teaspoon ground coriander
- Sea salt
- Freshly ground black pepper

Directions:
1. In a large saucepan, warm the oil over medium-high heat.
2. Add the onions, celery, carrots, and garlic and sauté until softened, 5 to 7 minutes.
3. Stir in the beans, lentils, and vegetable broth and bring the mixture to a boil. Reduce the heat to low and simmer 10 minutes.
4. Stir in the tomatoes, greens, oregano, and coriander and simmer until the greens are tender, about 5 minutes.
5. Season the cassoulet with salt and pepper and serve.

Nutrition Info:
- Info Per Serving: Calories: 446 ; Fat:4 g ;Saturated fat: 1 g ;Sodium: 127 mg

Butternut Squash, Bulgur, And Tempeh Burritos

Servings: X
Cooking Time: 15 Minutes

Ingredients:
- 1 teaspoon olive oil
- 1 cup chopped butternut squash
- ½ cup chopped onion
- ½ cup cooked bulgur
- ½ cup crumbled tempeh
- ½ teaspoon chili powder
- ¼ teaspoon ground cumin
- 4 (6-inch) whole-grain tortillas
- ½ cup low-sodium tomato or mango salsa
- 1 scallion, white and green parts, sliced
- ½ cup shredded lettuce
- ¼ cup fat-free sour cream

Directions:
1. In a medium skillet, warm the olive oil over medium-high heat.
2. Add the squash and onions and sauté until tender, 8 to 10 minutes.
3. Add the bulgur, tempeh, chili powder, and cumin and sauté until the bulgur is heated through, about 7 minutes.
4. Wrap the tortillas in a clean kitchen towel and heat in the microwave for 15 to 30 seconds.
5. Lay the tortillas out and evenly divide the squash mixture between them. Top each with the salsa, scallion, lettuce, and sour cream.
6. Wrap the tortillas around the filling and serve.

Nutrition Info:
- Info Per Serving: Calories: 423 ; Fat: 13 g ;Saturated fat: 2 g ;Sodium: 712 mg

Farro Sloppy Joes

Servings: X
Cooking Time: 20 Minutes

Ingredients:
- ¾ cup uncooked pearled farro, rinsed well
- 1 cup water
- 1 teaspoon olive oil
- 1 red bell pepper, chopped
- ½ cup sweet onion, finely chopped
- 1 teaspoon minced garlic
- 1 (15-ounce) can low-sodium diced tomatoes, with their juices
- 1 teaspoon maple syrup
- 1 teaspoon low-sodium tamari sauce
- ½ teaspoon chili powder
- ¼ teaspoon dry mustard
- ¼ teaspoon dried oregano
- 2 whole-grain hamburger rolls, for serving

Directions:
1. In a small saucepan, combine the farro with the water. Bring to a boil over high heat and then reduce the heat to low. Cover and simmer until the water is absorbed, 15 to 20 minutes. Drain any excess water.
2. While the farro is cooking, warm the oil in a medium skillet and sauté the bell pepper, onions, and garlic until softened, about 3 minutes.
3. Stir in the tomatoes, maple syrup, tamari, chili powder, mustard, and oregano and bring the sauce to a boil. Reduce the heat to low and simmer for 5 to 7 minutes, stirring occasionally.
4. Remove the sauce from the heat and stir in the cooked farro.
5. Divide the sloppy joe mixture between the rolls and serve.

Nutrition Info:
- Info Per Serving: Calories: 407 ; Fat: 6 g ;Saturated fat: 1 g ;Sodium: 282 mg

Spinach-ricotta Omelet

Servings: 4
Cooking Time: X

Ingredients:
- 1 (10-ounce) package frozen chopped spinach, thawed and drained
- ½ cup part-skim ricotta cheese
- 2 tablespoons grated Parmesan cheese
- 1/8 teaspoon nutmeg
- 7 egg whites
- 1 egg yolk
- ¼ cup milk
- 1/8 teaspoon pepper
- 1 tablespoon olive oil
- ¼ cup finely chopped onion

Directions:
1. Press spinach between layers of paper towel to remove all excess moisture. Set aside. In small bowl, combine ricotta with Parmesan cheese and nutmeg; set aside.
2. In medium bowl, beat egg whites until a soft foam forms. In small bowl, combine egg yolk with milk and pepper and beat well.
3. Heat a nonstick skillet over medium heat. Add olive oil, then add spinach and onion; cook and stir until onion is crisp-tender, about 4 minutes. Meanwhile, fold egg-yolk mixture into beaten egg whites. Add egg mixture to skillet; cook, running spatula around edges to let uncooked mixture flow underneath, until eggs are set but still moist.
4. Spoon ricotta mixture on top of eggs; cover pan, and let cook for 2 minutes. Then fold omelet and serve immediately.

Nutrition Info:
- Info Per Serving: Calories: 162.81; Fat:8.74 g ;Saturated fat: 3.23 g ;Sodium: 245.82 mg

Stuffed Mushrooms

Servings: 4
Cooking Time: 10 Min

Ingredients:
- 4 large portobello mushrooms, stems removed
- 1 tbsp. avocado oil
- 1 (15 oz) can low-sodium garbanzo beans, drained and rinsed
- 1 cup wild rice, cooked
- ½ medium red bell pepper, seeds removed and finely chopped
- ½ cup red cabbage, finely chopped
- Himalayan pink salt
- Ground black pepper

Directions:
1. Heat the oven to 350°F gas mark 4.
2. Place the portobello mushrooms gill side down on a large baking sheet and drizzle with avocado oil.
3. Bake for 10 minutes, flip, and bake for another 10 minutes, until tender. Remove and leave the oven on.
4. In a large-sized mixing bowl, add the garbanzo beans, wild rice, red bell pepper, and red cabbage, season with salt and pepper to taste.
5. Divide the mixture into each portobello mushroom cup. Return to the oven and bake for 10 minutes until heated through. Remove from the oven and serve warm.

Nutrition Info:
- Info Per Serving: Calories: 194 ; Fat: 6 g ;Saturated fat: 1 g ;Sodium: 181 mg

Corn-and-chili Pancakes

Servings: 6
Cooking Time: X

Ingredients:
- ½ cup buttermilk
- 1 tablespoon olive oil
- ½ cup egg substitute
- ½ cup grated extra-sharp Cheddar cheese
- 1 jalapeño pepper, minced
- 2 ears sweet corn
- ½ cup cornmeal
- 1 cup all-purpose flour
- 1½ teaspoons baking powder
- ½ teaspoon baking soda
- 1 tablespoon sugar
- 1 tablespoon chili powder
- 1 tablespoon peanut oil
- 1 tablespoon butter

Directions:
1. In large bowl, combine buttermilk, olive oil, egg substitute, Cheddar, and jalapeño pepper and mix well.
2. Cut the kernels off the sweet corn and add to buttermilk mixture along with cornmeal, flour, baking powder, baking soda, sugar, and chili powder; mix until combined. Let stand for 10 minutes.
3. Heat griddle or frying pan over medium heat. Brush with the butter, then add the batter, ¼ cup at a time. Cook until bubbles form and start to break and sides look dry, about 3–4 minutes. Carefully flip pancakes and cook until light golden brown on second side, about 2–3 minutes. Serve immediately.

Nutrition Info:
- Info Per Serving: Calories:252.62; Fat: 9.20 g ;Saturated fat:3.03 g ;Sodium:287.01 mg

Smoky Bean And Lentil Chili

Servings: X
Cooking Time: 30 Minutes

Ingredients:
- 1 teaspoon olive oil
- 1 red bell pepper, diced
- ¼ cup chopped sweet onion
- 1 teaspoon minced garlic
- 2 tablespoons chili powder
- 1 teaspoon smoked sweet paprika
- 1 cup low-sodium canned black beans, rinsed and drained
- 1 cup low-sodium canned lentils, rinsed and drained
- 1 cup shelled edamame
- 1 cup low-sodium canned diced tomatoes, drained
- ½ cup corn kernels
- ½ diced avocado, for garnish

Directions:
1. In a large saucepan, warm the olive oil over medium-high heat.
2. Add the bell pepper, onions, and garlic and sauté until softened, about 4 minutes. Stir in the chili powder and paprika and sauté 1 minute.
3. Stir in the black beans, lentils, edamame, tomatoes, and corn and lower the heat to medium. Cook, stirring occasionally, until the chili is hot and fragrant, about 25 minutes.
4. Serve topped with avocado.

Nutrition Info:
- Info Per Serving: Calories: 512 ; Fat: 16 g ;Saturated fat: 2 g ;Sodium: 105 mg

Butter Bean Rotini

Servings: 4
Cooking Time: 15 Min

Ingredients:
- 8 oz rotini pasta
- 2 tbsp. avocado oil
- 1 bunch spinach, stemmed and chopped
- 1 (15 oz) can low-sodium diced tomatoes, drained
- 1 (15 oz) can low-sodium butter beans, drained and rinsed
- 1 tsp thyme, chopped
- 1 tsp oregano, chopped
- Fine sea salt
- Ground black pepper

Directions:
1. Fill a large stockpot with water and bring to the boil.
2. Cook the pasta for 8 minutes or according to the package instructions until al dente. Remove from the heat and reserve ¼ cup of the pasta water and drain the remaining water.
3. In a large heavy-bottom pan, heat the avocado oil over medium heat until hot.
4. Add the spinach and fry for 4 to 6 minutes, or until wilted.
5. Add the tomatoes and butter beans, cook for 3 to 5 minutes, or until heated through and the tomatoes have released some of their water.
6. Season with thyme, oregano, salt and pepper.
7. Mix the cooked pasta into the pan along with the reserved water. Cook for 1 minute until heated through and starting to thicken.

Nutrition Info:
- Info Per Serving: Calories: 435 ; Fat: 9 g ;Saturated fat: 1 g ;Sodium: 208 mg

Risotto With Artichokes

Servings: 6
Cooking Time: X

Ingredients:
- 2 cups water
- 2½ cups low-sodium vegetable broth
- 2 tablespoons olive oil
- 4 shallots, minced
- 3 cloves garlic, minced
- 1 (10-ounce) box frozen artichoke hearts, thawed
- 1½ cups Arborio rice
- 1/8 teaspoon pepper
- ¼ cup grated Parmesan cheese
- 1 tablespoon butter
- ½ cup chopped fresh basil leaves

Directions:
1. In medium saucepan, combine water and broth; heat over low heat until warm; keep on heat.
2. In large saucepan, heat olive oil over medium heat. Add shallots and garlic; cook and stir until crisp-tender, about 4 minutes. Add artichokes; cook and stir for 3 minutes.
3. Add rice; cook and stir for 2 minutes. Add the broth mixture, a cup at a time, stirring until the liquid is absorbed, about 20–25 minutes. Stir in pepper, Parmesan, butter, and basil; cover and let stand for 5 minutes off the heat. Serve immediately.

Nutrition Info:
- Info Per Serving: Calories:317.17 ; Fat: 8.90 g ;Saturated fat:2.86g ;Sodium: 223.71 mg

Pumpkin And Chickpea Patties

Servings: X
Cooking Time: 20 Minutes

Ingredients:
- 2 teaspoons olive oil, divided
- 2 cups grated fresh pumpkin
- ½ cup grated carrot
- ½ teaspoon minced garlic
- 2 cups low-sodium chickpeas, rinsed and drained
- ½ cup ground almonds
- 2 large egg whites
- 1 scallion, white and green parts, chopped
- ½ teaspoon chopped fresh thyme
- Sea salt
- Freshly ground black pepper

Directions:
1. Preheat the oven to 400°F.
2. Line a baking sheet with parchment paper and set aside.
3. In a large skillet, heat ½ teaspoon olive oil over medium-high heat. Add the pumpkin, carrots, and garlic and sauté until softened, about 4 minutes. Remove from the heat and transfer to a food processor. Wipe the skillet clean with paper towels.
4. Add the chickpeas, almonds, egg whites, scallions, and thyme to the food processor. Pulse until the mixture holds together when pressed.
5. Season with salt and pepper and divide the pumpkin mixture into 8 equal patties, flattening them to about ½-inch thick.
6. Heat the remaining 1½ teaspoons olive oil in the skillet. Cook the patties until lightly browned, about 4 minutes on each side.
7. Place the skillet in the oven and bake for an additional 5 minutes, until the patties are completely heated through.
8. Serve.

Nutrition Info:
- Info Per Serving: Calories: 560 ; Fat: 25 g ;Saturated fat: 3 g ;Sodium: 62 mg

Kidney Bean Stew

Servings: 4
Cooking Time: 25 Min

Ingredients:
- 2 tsp avocado oil
- 1 leek, thinly sliced
- ½ brown onion, finely chopped
- 1 tsp garlic, minced
- 3 cups low-sodium vegetable stock
- 1 cup Roma tomatoes, chopped
- 2 medium carrots, peeled and thinly sliced
- 1 cup cauliflower florets
- 1 cup broccoli florets
- 1 green bell pepper, seeds removed and diced
- 1 cup low-sodium canned kidney beans, rinsed and drained
- Pinch red pepper flakes
- Himalayan pink salt
- Ground black pepper
- 2 tbsp. low-fat Parmesan cheese, grated for garnish
- 1 tbsp. parsley, chopped for garnish

Directions:
1. In a large-sized stockpot, warm the avocado oil over medium-high heat.
2. Add the sliced leek, chopped onions, and minced garlic and fry for 4 minutes until softened.
3. Add the vegetable stock, tomatoes, carrots, cauliflower, broccoli, green bell peppers, kidney beans, and red pepper flakes, mix to combine.
4. Bring the stew to a boil, then reduce the heat to low and simmer for 18 to 20 minutes until the vegetables are tender.
5. Season with salt and pepper to taste.
6. Top with Parmesan cheese and parsley.

Nutrition Info:
- Info Per Serving: Calories:270 ; Fat: 8g ;Saturated fat: 3g ;Sodium: 237 mg

Cauliflower, Green Pea, And Wild Rice Pilaf

Servings: X
Cooking Time: 45 Minutes

Ingredients:
- 2 teaspoons olive oil
- ½ small sweet onion, chopped
- 1 teaspoon minced garlic
- 1 cup wild rice
- 3½ cups low-sodium vegetable broth
- 1 cup small cauliflower florets
- 1 cup frozen green peas
- ½ cup low-sodium canned lentils, rinsed and drained
- 1 teaspoon chopped fresh thyme
- 2 tablespoons sunflower seeds

Directions:
1. In a large skillet, warm the olive oil over medium-high heat.
2. Add the onions and garlic and sauté until softened, about 3 minutes.
3. Stir in the rice and broth and bring to a boil. Reduce the heat to low, cover, and let simmer until most of the liquid is absorbed and the rice is tender, about 45 minutes.
4. While the rice is cooking, place a medium saucepan filled with water over high heat and bring to a boil. Add the cauliflower and peas and blanch until tender-crisp, about 5 minutes. Drain and set aside.
5. When the rice is cooked, stir in the lentils, cauliflower, peas, thyme, and sunflower seeds.
6. Serve.

Nutrition Info:
- Info Per Serving: Calories: 565 ; Fat: 9 g ;Saturated fat: 1 g ;Sodium: 150 mg

Pinto Bean Tortillas

Servings: 4
Cooking Time: 25 Min

Ingredients:
- 1 (15 oz) can low-sodium pinto beans, rinsed and drained
- ¼ cup canned fire-roasted tomato salsa
- ¾ cup dairy-free cheddar cheese, shredded and divided
- 1 medium red bell pepper, seeded, chopped and divided
- 2 tbsp. olive oil, divided
- 4 large, wholegrain tortillas

Directions:
1. Place the drained pinto beans and the tomato salsa together in a food processor. Process until smooth.
2. Spread ½ cup of the pinto bean mixture on each tortilla. Sprinkle each tortilla with 3 tbsp. of dairy-free cheddar cheese and ¼ cup of red bell pepper. Fold in half and repeat with the remaining tortillas.
3. Add 1 tbsp. of olive oil to a large, heavy-bottom pan over medium heat until hot. Place the first two folded tortillas in the pan. Cover and cook for 2 minutes until the tortillas are crispy on the bottom. Flip and cook for 2 minutes until crispy on the other side.
4. Repeat with the remaining folded tortillas and the remaining olive oil. Keep warm until ready to serve.

Nutrition Info:
- Info Per Serving: Calories:438 ; Fat: 21 g ;Saturated fat: 5 g ;Sodium: 561 mg

Spaghetti Squash Skillet

Servings: X
Cooking Time: 35 Minutes

Ingredients:
- 1 (2-pound) spaghetti squash
- 1 tablespoon olive oil, divided
- Sea salt
- Freshly ground black pepper
- ½ cup chopped sweet onion
- 1 teaspoon minced garlic
- 1 orange bell pepper, diced
- 16 asparagus spears, woody ends trimmed, cut into 2-inch pieces
- ½ cup sliced sun-dried tomatoes
- 2 cups shredded kale
- 1 tablespoon chopped fresh basil

Directions:
1. Preheat the oven to 400°F.
2. Line a baking sheet with parchment paper and set aside.
3. Slice the squash in half lengthwise and scoop out the seeds. Place the squash, cut-side up, on the baking sheet. Brush the cut edges and hollows with 1 teaspoon olive oil and season lightly with salt and pepper.
4. Roast the squash until a knife can be inserted easily into the thickest section, 30 to 35 minutes.
5. Remove from the oven and let the squash cool for 10 minutes, then use a fork to shred the flesh into a medium bowl. Set aside.
6. While the squash is cooling, warm the remaining 2 teaspoons olive oil in a medium skillet over medium heat. Add the onions and garlic and sauté until softened, about 3 minutes.
7. Stir in the bell pepper, asparagus, sun-dried tomatoes, and kale and sauté until the vegetables and greens are tender, about 5 minutes.
8. Add the shredded spaghetti squash and basil and toss to combine.
9. Serve.

Nutrition Info:
- Info Per Serving: Calories: 340 ; Fat:10 g ;Saturated fat: 2 g ;Sodium: 287 mg

Quinoa With Spinach And Artichokes

Servings: 6
Cooking Time: X

Ingredients:
- 2 tablespoons olive oil
- 1 onion, chopped
- 4 cloves garlic, minced
- 1 (10-ounce) package frozen spinach, thawed and drained
- 1 (10-ounce) package frozen artichoke hearts, thawed and drained
- 1 cup quinoa
- 2½ cups low-sodium vegetable broth
- 2 tablespoons lemon juice
- 1/8 teaspoon pepper
- 1 teaspoon fresh oregano leaves

Directions:
1. In large saucepan, combine olive oil, onion, and garlic over medium heat; cook and stir until tender, about 5 minutes. Add spinach and artichokes; cook and stir until most of the liquid evaporates.
2. Stir in quinoa, then add vegetable broth. Bring to a simmer, then reduce heat to low. Cover and cook for 8 minutes, then uncover and cook, stirring, until quinoa is tender, about 4–5 minutes longer.
3. Stir in lemon juice, pepper, and oregano leaves and serve immediately.

Nutrition Info:
- Info Per Serving: Calories: 226.63; Fat:7.41 g ;Saturated fat:1.07 g ;Sodium:206.13 mg

Tofu And Root Vegetable Curry

Servings: X
Cooking Time: 25 Minutes

Ingredients:
- 2 teaspoons olive oil
- 1 cup small cauliflower florets
- 1 parsnip, diced
- 1 carrot, diced
- 1 red bell pepper, thinly sliced
- 1 cup diced sweet potato
- 1 teaspoon peeled, grated fresh ginger
- ½ teaspoon minced garlic
- 1 cup low-sodium vegetable broth
- 2 tomatoes, chopped
- 2 cups diced extra-firm tofu
- 2 tablespoons curry powder or paste
- ¼ cup chopped cashews, for garnish

Directions:
1. In a large saucepan, warm the olive oil over medium-high heat.
2. Add the cauliflower, parsnips, carrots, bell peppers, sweet potatoes, ginger, and garlic and sauté until the vegetables begin to soften, about 10 minutes.
3. Stir in the vegetable broth, tomatoes, tofu, and curry powder and bring the mixture to a boil.
4. Reduce the heat to low and simmer until the vegetables are tender and everything is completely heated through, 15 to 18 minutes.
5. Serve topped with cashews.

Nutrition Info:
- Info Per Serving: Calories: 457 ; Fat: 20 g ;Saturated fat: 3 g ;Sodium: 135 mg

Spanish Omelet

Servings: 4
Cooking Time: X

Ingredients:
- 2 tablespoons olive oil, divided
- 1 onion, minced
- 2 cloves garlic, minced
- 1 stalk celery, chopped
- ½ cup chopped red bell pepper
- 1 jalapeño pepper, minced
- ½ teaspoon dried oregano
- 2 tomatoes, chopped
- 1/8 teaspoon salt
- 1/8 teaspoon pepper
- 1 egg
- 8 egg whites
- ¼ cup skim milk
- 2 tablespoons low-fat sour cream
- ½ cup grated extra-sharp Cheddar cheese

Directions:
1. For the sauce, in a small saucepan heat 1 tablespoon olive oil over medium heat. Add onion, garlic, celery, bell pepper, and jalapeño pepper; cook and stir for 4 minutes until crisp-tender. Add oregano, tomatoes, salt, and pepper, and bring to a simmer. Reduce heat to low and simmer for 5 minutes.
2. In large bowl, combine egg, egg whites, skim milk, and sour cream and beat until combined. Heat 1 tablespoon olive oil in nonstick skillet and add egg mixture. Cook, moving spatula around pan and lifting to let uncooked mixture flow underneath, until eggs are set but still moist.
3. Sprinkle with Cheddar and top with half of the tomato sauce. Cover and cook for 2–4 minutes longer, until bottom of omelet is golden brown. Fold over, slide onto serving plate, top with remaining tomato sauce, and serve.

Nutrition Info:
- Info Per Serving: Calories: 219.98; Fat:14.03 g ;Saturated fat: 4.95 g ;Sodium: 316.92 mg

Portobello Burgers

Servings: 4
Cooking Time: 25 Min

Ingredients:
- Aluminium foil
- 3 tbsp. avocado oil
- 1 tbsp. garlic, crushed
- 4 large portobello mushrooms, stems removed
- 4 crusty whole-grain rolls
- ½ cup dairy-free cheddar cheese, shredded
- Ground black pepper
- 4 iceberg lettuce leaves

Directions:
1. Heat the oven to 425°F gas mark 7. Line a baking sheet with aluminum foil.
2. In a small-sized mixing bowl, add the avocado oil and garlic, mix to combine. Brush half of the garlic mixture on both sides of the portobello mushrooms and let them sit for 10 minutes.
3. Meanwhile, cut the rolls open. Drizzle the remaining garlic mixture onto the bottom half of each roll. Place 2 tbsp. of cheddar cheese on each bottom half roll.
4. Place the mushrooms on the prepared baking sheet, cap-side down, and roast for 12 minutes on each side.
5. Put one portobello mushroom on the bottom of each roll, on top of the cheddar cheese. Season with ground black pepper and top with 1 lettuce leaf. Place the top bun on the lettuce leaf and serve. Repeat for the remaining mushrooms.

Nutrition Info:
- Info Per Serving: Calories: 307 ; Fat: 17 g ;Saturated fat: 5 g ;Sodium: 276 mg

Pumpkin Soufflé

Servings: 4
Cooking Time: X

Ingredients:
- 1 tablespoon olive oil
- 1 onion, chopped
- 4 cloves garlic, minced
- 1 (13-ounce) can solid-pack pumpkin
- 1 egg yolk
- 2 teaspoons chopped fresh thyme
- 4 egg whites
- 1/8 teaspoon salt
- ¼ teaspoon cream of tartar
- 2 tablespoons grated Parmesan cheese

Directions:
1. Preheat oven to 425°F. Grease the bottom of a 1-quart soufflé dish with peanut oil and set aside. In small saucepan, heat olive oil over medium heat. Add onion and garlic; cook and stir until tender, about 5 minutes.
2. Place in large bowl and let cool for 10 minutes. Blend in pumpkin, egg yolk, and thyme until smooth.
3. In medium bowl, combine egg whites, salt, and cream of tartar and beat until stiff peaks form. Stir a spoonful of the beaten egg whites into pumpkin mixture, then fold in remaining egg whites along with the Parmesan cheese. Pour into prepared soufflé dish.
4. Bake for 15 minutes, then reduce heat to 350°F and bake for another 20–25 minutes or until soufflé is puffed and golden brown. Serve immediately.

Nutrition Info:
- Info Per Serving: Calories: 118.83; Fat:5.74 g ;Saturated fat: 1.56 g ;Sodium:183.15 mg

Spaghetti Sauce

Servings: 6
Cooking Time: X

Ingredients:
- 2 tablespoons olive oil
- 1 onion, chopped
- 4 cloves garlic, minced
- 1 cup chopped celery
- 1 (8-ounce) package sliced mushrooms
- 1 (6-ounce) can no-salt tomato paste
- 2 (14-ounce) cans no-salt diced tomatoes, undrained
- 1 tablespoon dried Italian seasoning
- ½ cup grated carrots
- 1/8 teaspoon white pepper
- ½ cup dry red wine
- ½ cup water

Directions:
1. In large saucepan, heat olive oil over medium heat. Add onion and garlic; cook and stir until crisp-tender, about 4 minutes. Add celery and mushrooms; cook and stir for 2–3 minutes longer.
2. Add tomato paste; let paste brown a bit without stirring (this adds flavor to the sauce). Then add remaining ingredients and stir gently but thoroughly.
3. Bring sauce to a simmer, then reduce heat to low and partially cover. Simmer for 60–70 minutes, stirring occasionally, until sauce is blended and thickened. Serve over hot cooked pasta, couscous, or rice.

Nutrition Info:
- Info Per Serving: Calories: 155.73; Fat:5.11 g ;Saturated fat:0.72 g ;Sodium: 84.74 mg

Spaghetti With Creamy Tomato Sauce

Servings: 6–8
Cooking Time: X

Ingredients:
- 1 recipe Spaghetti Sauce
- ½ cup fat-free half-and-half
- 1 (16-ounce) package whole-grain pasta
- ½ cup grated Parmesan cheese

Directions:
1. Bring large pot of water to a boil. Prepare Spaghetti Sauce as directed. During last 5 minutes of cooking time, stir in light cream and stir to blend.
2. Cook pasta in boiling water according to package directions until al dente. Drain and add to Spaghetti Sauce; cook and stir for 1 minute to let the pasta absorb some of the sauce. Sprinkle with Parmesan and serve immediately.

Nutrition Info:
- Info Per Serving: Calories: 354.63; Fat:6.65 g ;Saturated fat:1.90 g ;Sodium:188.68 mg

Quinoa-stuffed Peppers

Servings: 6
Cooking Time: X

Ingredients:
- 1 recipe Quinoa Pepper Pilaf
- ½ cup chopped flat-leaf parsley
- 1 cup shredded Havarti cheese
- 6 large red bell peppers
- 2 cups Spaghetti Sauce

Directions:
1. Preheat oven to 350ºF. Prepare pilaf and fluff. Stir in parsley and Havarti. Cut tops from peppers and remove seeds and membranes.
2. Spray 9″ × 13″ baking dish with nonstick cooking spray. Place a layer of Spaghetti Sauce in the dish. Stuff peppers with pilaf and arrange on sauce. Pour remaining sauce over and around peppers.
3. Bake for 50–60 minutes or until peppers are tender. Serve immediately.

Nutrition Info:
- Info Per Serving: Calories: 406.04 ; Fat:15.40 g ;Saturated fat: 4.69 g ;Sodium: 468.06 mg

Chili-sautéed Tofu With Almonds

Servings: X
Cooking Time: 15 Minutes

Ingredients:
- 2 teaspoons olive oil
- ½ jalapeño pepper, chopped
- 1 teaspoon grated fresh ginger
- 1 teaspoon minced garlic
- 12 ounces extra-firm tofu, drained and cut into
- 1-inch cubes
- 2 cups shredded bok choy
- 1 red bell pepper, thinly sliced
- 1 scallion, white and green parts, thinly sliced
- 1 tablespoon low-sodium tamari sauce
- 1 tablespoon freshly squeezed lime juice
- 1 cup cooked quinoa, for serving
- ¼ cup chopped almonds, for garnish

Directions:
1. In a large skillet, warm the olive oil over medium-high heat.
2. Add the jalapeño, ginger, and garlic and sauté until softened, about 4 minutes.
3. Add the tofu, bok choy, bell peppers, and scallions and sauté until the tofu is lightly browned and the vegetables are tender, 8 to 10 minutes.
4. Stir in the tamari sauce and lime juice and toss to coat the ingredients.
5. Serve over quinoa, topped with chopped almonds.

Nutrition Info:
- Info Per Serving: Calories: 469 ; Fat: 24 g ;Saturated fat: 2 g ;Sodium: 279 mg

Desserts And Treats

Desserts And Treats

Silken Chocolate Mousse

Servings: 6
Cooking Time: X

Ingredients:
- 2 (1-ounce) squares unsweetened chocolate
- 2 tablespoons butter
- ½ cup sugar
- 1 teaspoon vanilla
- ½ cup satin or silken soft tofu
- 1 cup chocolate frozen yogurt
- 1 cup frozen non-dairy whipped topping, thawed

Directions:
1. Chop chocolate and place in small microwave-safe bowl with the butter. Microwave on medium for 2–4 minutes, stirring twice during cooking time, until chocolate is melted and mixture is smooth. Stir in sugar until sugar dissolves.
2. In blender or food processor, place chocolate mixture and add vanilla and tofu. Blend or process until smooth. If necessary, let cool for 10–15 minutes or until lukewarm.
3. Then add the frozen yogurt and blend or process until smooth. Finally add the whipped topping and blend or process until just mixed. Spoon into serving glasses, cover, and chill for 4–6 hours before serving.

Nutrition Info:
- Info Per Serving: Calories: 219.73; Fat:12.12 g ;Saturated fat: 7.86 g;Sodium:78.14 mg

Maple-walnut Pots De Crème

Servings: X
Cooking Time: 5 Minutes

Ingredients:
- ½ cup unsweetened soy milk
- ¼ teaspoon pure vanilla extract
- 1½ teaspoons unflavored gelatin
- ½ cup fat-free vanilla Greek yogurt
- ½ cup low-fat buttermilk
- ⅓ cup maple syrup
- Pinch sea salt
- 2 tablespoons chopped walnuts, for garnish

Directions:
1. In a small saucepan, stir together the soy milk and vanilla over medium heat until just warmer than room temperature, about 2 minutes.
2. Stir in the gelatin and heat the mixture until scalded, but not boiling, about 3 minutes.
3. Remove the saucepan from the heat and set aside to cool for 10 minutes.
4. Whisk in the yogurt, buttermilk, maple syrup, and salt until well blended.
5. Pour the mixture into 2 (6-ounce) ramekins and chill, covered, in the refrigerator until completely set, at least 4 hours.
6. Serve topped with walnuts.

Nutrition Info:
- Info Per Serving: Calories: 301; Fat: 6g ;Saturated fat: 1g ;Sodium: 200 mg

Cinnamon And Walnut Baked Pears

Servings: 4
Cooking Time: 25 Minutes

Ingredients:
- 2 ripe Bosc pears, halved and cored
- ¼ teaspoon cinnamon
- 2 tablespoons crushed walnuts
- 2 teaspoons maple syrup

Directions:
1. Preheat the oven to 350°F. Line a baking sheet with parchment paper.
2. Place the pear halves on the prepared baking sheet, hollow-side up, and sprinkle with the cinnamon. Fill the hollow with the walnuts.
3. Bake the pears for 25 minutes.
4. Drizzle the pear halves with the maple syrup and enjoy immediately.

Nutrition Info:
- Info Per Serving: Calories: 171 ; Fat: 3g ;Saturated fat: 0g ;Sodium: 3mg

Chocolate Granola Pie

Servings: 12
Cooking Time: X

Ingredients:
- 3 tablespoons butter or margarine
- 2 (1-ounce) squares unsweetened chocolate, chopped
- ¼ cup brown sugar
- ½ cup dark corn syrup
- 2 teaspoons vanilla
- 1 egg
- 3 egg whites
- 2 cups Cinnamon Granola
- 1 Loco Pie Crust , unbaked

Directions:
1. Preheat oven to 350ºF. In large saucepan, combine butter and chocolate. Melt over low heat, stirring frequently, until smooth. Remove from heat and add brown sugar, corn syrup, vanilla, egg, and egg whites and beat well until blended.
2. Stir in granola and pour into pie crust. Bake for 40–50 minutes or until filling is set and pie crust is deep golden brown. Let cool completely and serve.

Nutrition Info:
- Info Per Serving: Calories: 384.56; Fat:14.45 g ;Saturated fat:4.65 g;Sodium:137.51 mg

Lemon Mousse

Servings: 4
Cooking Time: X

Ingredients:
- 1 (0.25-ounce) envelope unflavored gelatin
- ¼ cup cold water
- 1/3 cup lemon juice
- 2/3 cup pear nectar
- ¼ cup sugar, divided
- 1 teaspoon grated lemon zest
- 1 cup lemon yogurt
- 2 pasteurized egg whites
- ¼ teaspoon cream of tartar

Directions:
1. In microwave-safe glass measuring cup, combine gelatin and cold water; let stand for 5 minutes to soften gelatin. Stir in lemon juice, pear nectar, and 2 tablespoons sugar. Microwave on high for 1–2 minutes, stirring twice during cooking time, until sugar and gelatin completely dissolve; stir in lemon zest. Let cool for 30 minutes.
2. When gelatin mixture is cool to the touch, blend in the lemon yogurt. Then, in medium bowl, combine egg whites with cream of tartar; beat until soft peaks form. Gradually stir in remaining 2 tablespoons sugar, beating until stiff peaks form.
3. Fold gelatin mixture into egg whites until combined. Pour into serving glasses or goblets, cover, and chill until firm, about 4–6 hours.

Nutrition Info:
- Info Per Serving: Calories: 151.27; Fat: 0.65 g ;Saturated fat: 0.40 g;Sodium:65.70 mg

Cashew Butter Latte

Servings: 1
Cooking Time: 10 Min

Ingredients:
- ¼ cup unsalted cashew butter
- 1 tsp vanilla extract
- 1 tsp organic honey
- ½ tsp ground cinnamon, plus more if needed
- 1 cup unsweetened cashew milk, more if needed

Directions:
1. Add the espresso, cashew butter, vanilla extract, honey, and cinnamon into a medium-sized stockpot over medium heat, whisking occasionally until the cashew butter has melted.
2. Heat the cashew milk over low heat in a small-sized stockpot. When it is warm (not hot), whisk it vigorously by hand, or use a handheld beater, to make it foamy.
3. Pour the hot coffee mixture into a mug and top with the foamy milk.

Nutrition Info:
- Info Per Serving: Calories: 169 ; Fat: 3 g ;Saturated fat:2 g ;Sodium: 128 mg

Peach Melba Frozen Yogurt Parfaits

Servings: 4
Cooking Time: 5 Minutes

Ingredients:
- 2 tablespoons slivered almonds
- 1 tablespoon brown sugar
- 2 peaches, peeled and chopped (see Ingredient Tip)
- 1 cup fresh raspberries
- 2 cups no-sugar-added vanilla frozen yogurt
- 2 tablespoons peach jam
- 2 tablespoons raspberry jam or preserves

Directions:
1. In a small nonstick skillet over medium heat, combine the almonds and brown sugar.
2. Cook, stirring frequently, until the sugar melts and coats the almonds, about 3 to 4 minutes. Remove from the heat and put the almonds on a plate to cool.
3. To make the parfaits: In four parfait or wine glasses, layer each with the peaches, raspberries, frozen yogurt, peach jam, and raspberry jam. Top each glass with the caramelized almonds.

Nutrition Info:
- Info Per Serving: Calories: 263 ; Fat: 5 g ;Saturated fat: 1 g ;Sodium: 91 mg

Fruit Yoghurt Parfait

Servings: 2
Cooking Time: 20 Min

Ingredients:
- 2 cups plain Greek yogurt
- 1 banana, sliced
- ½ cup strawberries, sliced
- ¼ cup almonds, chopped
- ¼ cup unsalted sunflower seeds, roasted
- 2 tbsp. organic honey
- 1 tbsp. chia seeds, for garnish
- 1 tbsp. small dark chocolate chips, for garnish

Directions:
1. Divide the yoghurt between two serving bowls.
2. Evenly divide the banana, strawberries, almonds, and roasted sunflower seeds between the bowls.
3. Drizzle each bowl with 1 tbsp. of honey and top them with chia seeds and chocolate chips.
4. Serve cold.

Nutrition Info:
- Info Per Serving: Calories: 394 ; Fat: 18 g ;Saturated fat: 2 g ;Sodium: 57 mg

Blueberry Crumble

Servings: 5
Cooking Time: 20 Minutes

Ingredients:
- 3 tablespoons olive oil, plus extra for greasing the baking pan
- ½ cup chopped walnuts
- 1 cup pitted Medjool dates
- 1 cup steel-cut oats
- 1½ cups blueberries
- 1½ tablespoons honey

Directions:
1. Preheat the oven to 350°F. Lightly oil an 8-inch-square baking pan.
2. In a food processor or blender, pulse the walnuts until they are finely ground. Transfer to a medium bowl and set aside.
3. Place the dates in the food processor and pulse until they become a coarse paste. Transfer to the bowl and mix with the walnuts.
4. Add the oats and the olive oil to the bowl and mix until the mixture sticks together.
5. Press half of the oat mixture into the bottom of the prepared baking pan.
6. Spread the blueberries evenly over the oat mixture and drizzle with the honey. Top with the remaining half of the oat mixture.
7. Bake for 20 minutes until the berries are bubbly. Enjoy immediately.

Nutrition Info:
- Info Per Serving: Calories:375 ; Fat: 17 g ;Saturated fat: 2g ;Sodium: 2 mg

Raisin Chocolate Slices

Servings: 16
Cooking Time: 30 Min

Ingredients:
- Cooking spray
- 2 cups raisins
- 3 large free-range eggs
- 1 cup whole-wheat flour
- ½ cup unsweetened cocoa powder
- ¼ cup sunflower oil
- 1 teaspoon baking soda
- Pinch fine sea salt

Directions:
1. Heat the oven to 350°F gas mark 4. Coat a deep baking dish with cooking spray, set aside.
2. Bring a small stockpot of water to the boil and remove from the heat.
3. In a medium-sized mixing bowl, cover the raisins with the boiling water, soak for 15 minutes, drain.
4. In a food processor, add the raisins and 2 tbsp. of water, process until smooth.
5. Add the eggs, one at a time, mixing between each addition.
6. Add the flour, cocoa powder, sunflower oil, baking soda, and salt, mix until well combined.
7. Pour the batter into the prepared baking dish and bake for 30 minutes, or until the toothpick inserted comes out clean.
8. Remove from the oven and cool completely.

Nutrition Info:
- Info Per Serving: Calories: 125; Fat: 7 g ;Saturated fat: 1 g ;Sodium: 103 mg

Lite Creamy Cheesecake

Servings: 12
Cooking Time: X

Ingredients:
- 1½ cups crushed gingersnap crumbs
- 1/3 cup finely chopped walnuts
- 2 tablespoons butter or margarine, melted
- 2 tablespoons orange juice
- 1½ cups nonfat cottage cheese
- 1 cup sugar
- ¼ cup orange juice
- 2 tablespoons lemon juice
- 1 (8-ounce) package light cream cheese, softened 1 (3-ounce) package nonfat cream cheese, softened
- 1 cup nonfat sour cream
- 1 egg
- 3 egg whites
- ¼ cup cornstarch
- 1 tablespoon vanilla

Directions:
1. Preheat oven to 350°F. In medium bowl, combine gingersnap crumbs, walnuts, butter, and 2 tablespoons orange juice; mix until even. Press into bottom and up sides of 9″ springform pan; set aside in refrigerator.
2. In blender or food processor, combine cottage cheese, sugar, ¼ cup orange juice, and lemon juice; blend or process until very smooth. Scrape down sides and blend or process again.
3. In large mixing bowl, combine both packages of cream cheese and beat until smooth. Add sour cream; beat again until smooth. Add egg and beat well, then add cottage cheese mixture and beat well. Stir in egg whites, cornstarch, and vanilla and beat until smooth.
4. Pour cheese mixture into gingersnap crust. Bake for 50–60 minutes or until cheesecake is set around edges but still soft in center. Remove from oven and place on wire rack; let cool for 1 hour. Cover and refrigerate until cold, at least 4 hours.

Nutrition Info:
- Info Per Serving: Calories: 254.77; Fat: 9.11 g ;Saturated fat: 4.07 g;Sodium:206.98 mg

Pumpkin Pie Pudding

Servings: 4
Cooking Time: 5 Minutes

Ingredients:
- 1 tablespoon gelatin
- ¼ cup water
- 1 (12-ounce) can low-fat evaporated milk
- ½ cup pumpkin puree
- 1 tablespoon maple syrup
- 2 teaspoons cinnamon

Directions:
1. In a small bowl, sprinkle the gelatin over the water and set aside for 10 minutes.
2. In a medium saucepan over medium heat, stir together the evaporated milk, pumpkin puree, maple syrup, and cinnamon. Heat for about 5 minutes, or until it begins to foam.
3. Remove the pumpkin mixture from the heat and stir in the gelatin water.
4. Pour the pumpkin pie pudding through a fine sieve into four small (½-cup) ramekins, cover with plastic wrap, and refrigerate for 2 hours. Serve chilled.

Nutrition Info:
- Info Per Serving: Calories: 116 ; Fat: 2 g ;Saturated fat: 1g ;Sodium: 112 mg

Dark Chocolate Meringues

Servings: 18
Cooking Time: 15 Minutes

Ingredients:
- 2 egg whites, at room temperature
- ⅓ cup granulated sugar
- 3 tablespoons confectioner's sugar
- ¼ cup cocoa powder
- Pinch salt
- ½ teaspoon vanilla extract
- ¼ cup mini semisweet chocolate chips

Directions:
1. Preheat the oven to 350°F. Line a baking sheet with parchment paper and set aside.
2. In a clean, dry medium bowl, place the egg whites. Put the bowl inside a larger bowl filled with very warm water and let stand for 5 minutes to warm up the egg whites.
3. Remove the medium bowl from the large bowl and carefully dry the outside.
4. In another medium bowl, sift together the granulated sugar, powdered sugar, cocoa powder, and salt.
5. Start beating the egg whites and gradually add the sugar mixture, beating constantly, until the mixture stands in peaks that droop when you pull up the turned-off beater.
6. Fold in the vanilla extract and the chocolate chips.
7. Drop by tablespoons onto the prepared baking sheet.
8. Bake for 13 to 15 minutes or until the meringues are set. Cool on the baking sheet for 5 minutes, then remove to a wire rack to completely cool. Store in layers separated by wax paper in an airtight container at room temperature up to 3 days.

Nutrition Info:
- Info Per Serving: Calories: 35 ; Fat: 1 g ;Saturated fat: 1 g ;Sodium: 9 mg

Grapefruit Pie

Servings: 8–10
Cooking Time: X

Ingredients:
- 1 Loco Pie Crust , baked
- 2 small red grapefruits
- 1 (8-ounce) package low-fat cream cheese, softened
- 1 (14-ounce) can low-fat sweetened condensed milk
- 3 tablespoons honey

Directions:
1. Prepare crust according to directions and let cool completely. Cut one grapefruit in half and squeeze juice from one half. Peel other half and chop fruit; set aside.
2. In medium bowl, beat cream cheese until smooth; gradually add condensed milk, beating until fluffy. Add grapefruit juice and mix well; pour into crust and refrigerate.
3. Peel second grapefruit and separate into sections; remove seeds. Sprinkle chopped grapefruit over pie; arrange grapefruit sections on top. Drizzle with honey; cover and refrigerate for 4–6 hours before serving.

Nutrition Info:
- Info Per Serving: Calories: 349.21; Fat: 13.36 g ;Saturated fat:5.65 g;Sodium: 170.15 mg

Butterscotch Meringues

Servings: 30
Cooking Time: X

Ingredients:
- 3 egg whites Pinch of salt
- ¼ teaspoon cream of tartar
- 2/3 cup sugar
- 2 tablespoons brown sugar
- 10 round hard butterscotch candies, finely crushed

Directions:
1. Preheat oven to 250°F. In large bowl, beat egg whites with salt and cream of tartar until foamy. Gradually beat in sugar and brown sugar until stiff peaks form and sugar is dissolved. Fold in the finely crushed candies.
2. Drop by teaspoonfuls onto a baking sheet lined with aluminum foil or Silpat liners. Bake for 50–60 minutes or until meringues are set and crisp and very light golden brown. Cool on the cookie sheets for 3 minutes, then carefully peel off the foil and place on wire racks to cool.

Nutrition Info:
- Info Per Serving: Calories:29.39; Fat:0.06 g ;Saturated fat:0.04 g;Sodium: 17.97 mg

Strawberry-mango Meringue Pie

Servings: 8
Cooking Time: X

Ingredients:

- 1 teaspoon flour
- 3 egg whites
- ¼ teaspoon cream of tartar
- ½ cup sugar
- 1 teaspoon vanilla
- 1 (8-ounce) package low-fat cream cheese, softened
- 1 cup mango yogurt
- 1 cup chopped strawberries
- 2 mangoes, peeled and chopped

Directions:

1. Preheat oven to 300ºF. Spray a 9″ pie plate with nonstick cooking spray and dust with 1 teaspoon flour. In large bowl, combine egg whites and cream of tartar; beat until soft peaks form. Gradually beat in sugar until very stiff peaks form. Beat in vanilla. Spread into prepared pan, building up sides to form a shell.
2. Bake for 50–60 minutes or until shell is very light golden and dry to the touch. Turn oven off and let shell stand in oven for 1 hour. Cool completely.
3. For filling, in medium bowl beat cream cheese until fluffy. Gradually add yogurt, beating until well combined. Fold in strawberries and mangoes. Spoon into meringue pie shell, cover, and chill for 3–4 hours before serving.

Nutrition Info:

- Info Per Serving: Calories: 195.15; Fat:5.51 g ;Saturated fat: 3.40 g;Sodium:123.32 mg

Loco Pie Crust

Servings: 8
Cooking Time: X

Ingredients:

- ½ cup plus
- 1 tablespoon mayonnaise
- 3 tablespoons buttermilk
- 1 teaspoon vinegar
- 1½ cups flour

Directions:

1. In large bowl, combine mayonnaise, buttermilk, and vinegar and mix well. Add flour, stirring with a fork to form a ball. You may need to add more buttermilk or more flour to make a workable dough. Press dough into a ball, wrap in plastic wrap, and refrigerate for 1 hour.
2. When ready to bake, preheat oven to 400ºF. Roll out dough between two sheets of waxed paper. Remove top sheet and place crust in 9″ pie pan. Carefully ease off the top sheet of paper, then ease the crust into the pan and press to bottom and sides. Fold edges under and flute.
3. Either use as recipe directs, or bake for 5 minutes, then press crust down with fork if necessary. Bake for 5–8 minutes longer or until crust is light golden brown.

Nutrition Info:

- Info Per Serving: Calories:171.83; Fat: 7.35 g ;Saturated fat:1.18 g;Sodium: 65.46 mg

Choc Chip Banana Muffins

Servings: 8
Cooking Time: 20 Min

Ingredients:
- 2 tbsp. ground flaxseeds
- 5 tbsp. water
- 2 cups almond flour
- 1 tbsp. ground cinnamon
- 1 tsp baking powder
- 3 (1 cup) medium ripe bananas, mashed
- 2 tbsp. organic honey
- ¼ cup dark chocolate chips
- 1 tsp vanilla extract
- ¼ cup unsalted walnuts, chopped

Directions:
1. Heat the oven to 375°F gas mark 5. Line a muffin tin with 8 muffin cup liners. Set aside.
2. In a small-sized mixing bowl, stir in the flaxseeds and water and let this sit for 5 minutes until the mixture congeals.
3. In a large-sized mixing bowl, add the almond flour, cinnamon, and baking powder and mix to combine.
4. In a medium-sized mixing bowl, add the flaxseed mixture, bananas, honey, chocolate chips, and vanilla extract, mix to combine. Slowly pour the wet ingredients into the dry ingredients, mix well. Add in the walnuts and mix.
5. Spoon the mixture evenly into the 8 lined muffin tin, bake for 20 minutes, or until the inserted toothpick comes out clean.
6. Serve warm or once completely cooled, store in an airtight container to stay fresh.

Nutrition Info:
- Info Per Serving: Calories: 199 ; Fat: 5 g ;Saturated fat: 1 g ;Sodium: 64 mg

Chocolate Banana Caramel Pudding

Servings: 4
Cooking Time: 15 Minutes

Ingredients:
- 2 ripe bananas, cut into 1-inch chunks (see Ingredient Tip)
- ¼ cup cocoa powder, plus more to adjust chocolate level
- ¼ cup low-fat soy milk
- 2 tablespoons vanilla protein powder
- 2 tablespoons caramel sauce
- ½ teaspoon vanilla extract
- Pinch salt
- 2 tablespoons mini semisweet chocolate chips

Directions:
1. In a blender or food processor, combine the bananas, cocoa powder, soy milk, protein powder, caramel sauce, vanilla, and salt, and blend or process until smooth.
2. Add more cocoa, about a tablespoon at a time, if you'd like a darker chocolate pudding or to adjust the chocolate flavor.
3. Pour into 4 small cups and top each with the chocolate chips, then serve. Or you can cover the puddings and chill for 2 to 3 hours before serving.

Nutrition Info:
- Info Per Serving: Calories: 164 ; Fat: 4 g ;Saturated fat: 2 g ;Sodium: 29 mg

Sweet Potato And Chocolate Muffins

Servings: 12
Cooking Time: 25 Minutes

Ingredients:
- ¾ cup mashed, cooked sweet potato
- ½ cup soy milk
- ½ cup brown sugar
- ⅓ cup canola oil
- 2 large eggs
- 1¾ cups whole-wheat flour
- ¾ cup rolled oats
- 1½ teaspoons baking powder
- ¾ teaspoon baking soda
- ¼ teaspoon ground cinnamon
- ¼ teaspoon ground nutmeg
- ½ cup mini dark chocolate chips

Directions:
1. Preheat the oven to 350°F.
2. Line 12 muffin cups with paper liners and set aside.
3. In a medium bowl, whisk together the sweet potato, soy milk, brown sugar, canola oil, and eggs until well blended.
4. In a large bowl, stir together the flour, oats, baking powder, baking soda, cinnamon, nutmeg, and chocolate chips.
5. Add the wet ingredients to the dry ingredients and stir until just combined. Spoon the batter into the prepared muffin cups, filling each cup about two-thirds full.
6. Place the muffins in the oven and bake until a toothpick inserted in the center comes out clean, about 25 minutes.
7. Store in an airtight container in the refrigerator for up to 5 days, or freeze for up to 3 months.

Nutrition Info:
- Info Per Serving: Calories: 242 ; Fat: 10 g ;Saturated fat: 3 g ;Sodium: 104 mg

Oatmeal Brownies

Servings: 16
Cooking Time: X

Ingredients:
- ¼ cup prune puree
- ¼ cup finely chopped dates
- ½ cup all-purpose flour
- ½ cup ground oatmeal
- ½ cup cocoa powder
- ½ teaspoon baking soda
- ½ cup brown sugar
- ¼ cup sugar
- 1 egg
- 1 egg white
- ¼ cup chocolate yogurt
- 2 teaspoons vanilla
- 2 tablespoons butter or plant sterol margarine, melted
- ½ cup dark-chocolate chips

Directions:
1. Preheat oven to 350°F. Spray an 8″ square baking pan with nonstick cooking spray containing flour and set aside.
2. In small bowl, combine prune puree and dates; mix well and set aside. In large bowl, combine flour, oatmeal, cocoa, baking soda, brown sugar, and sugar, and mix well.
3. Add egg, egg white, yogurt, vanilla, and butter to prune mixture and mix well. Add to flour mixture and stir just until blended. Spoon into prepared pan and smooth top. Bake for 22–30 minutes or until edges are set but the center is still slightly soft. Remove from oven and place on wire rack.
4. In microwave-safe bowl, place chocolate chips. Microwave on 50 percent power for 1 minute, then remove and stir. Microwave for 30 seconds longer, then stir. If necessary, repeat microwave process until chips are melted. Pour over warm brownies and gently spread to cover. Let cool completely and cut into bars.

Nutrition Info:
- Info Per Serving: Calories:153.83; Fat: 4.88 g ;Saturated fat:2.63 g;Sodium:63.58 mg

Sweetato Bundt Cake

Servings: 12
Cooking Time: 45 Min

Ingredients:
- Cooking spray
- ¾ cup sweet potato, cooked and mashed
- ½ cup almond milk
- ½ cup brown sugar
- ⅓ cup sunflower oil
- 2 large free-range eggs
- 1¾ cups whole-wheat flour
- ¾ cup quick oats
- 1½ tsp baking powder
- ¾ tsp baking soda
- ¼ tsp ground cinnamon
- ¼ tsp ground nutmeg
- ¼ tsp ground allspice
- ½ cup dark chocolate chips

Directions:
1. Preheat the oven to 350°F gas mark 4.
2. Coat a Bundt cake pan with cooking spray and set aside.
3. In a stand mixer, add the mashed sweet potato, almond milk, sugar, sunflower oil, and eggs, beat until well blended.
4. In a large-sized mixing bowl, add the flour, oats, baking powder, baking soda cinnamon, nutmeg, allspice, and dark chocolate chips, mix to combine.
5. With the stand mixer on low, add 1 soup spoonful at a time of the dry ingredients into the wet ingredients, beat until well combined.
6. Spoon the batter into the prepared Bundt cake pan. Bake for 45 minutes, or until the toothpick inserted comes out clean.
7. Serve or store in an airtight container to stay fresh.

Nutrition Info:
- Info Per Serving: Calories: 242 ; Fat: 10g ;Saturated fat: 3 g ;Sodium: 104 mg

Dark Chocolate Brownie Bites

Servings: 12
Cooking Time: 18 Minutes

Ingredients:
- ¼ cup salted butter, melted
- ¼ cup puréed beets
- ½ cup packed brown sugar
- 3 tablespoons honey
- 1 teaspoon vanilla extract
- 1 egg
- 1 egg white
- Pinch salt
- ¼ teaspoon baking powder
- ½ cup whole-wheat flour
- ¼ cup all-purpose flour
- ⅓ cup cocoa powder

Directions:
1. Preheat the oven to 350°F. Line 24 mini muffin cups with mini paper liners and set aside.
2. In a medium bowl, combine the butter, beets, brown sugar, honey, and vanilla and mix well.
3. Add the egg and the egg white and beat until smooth.
4. In a separate medium bowl, combine the salt, baking powder, whole-wheat flour, all-purpose flour, and cocoa powder. Stir the dry ingredients into the butter-sugar mixture just until combined.
5. Spoon the batter among the prepared muffin cups, filling each about ⅔ full. Each cup should take about 1 tablespoon of batter.
6. Bake for 16 to 18 minutes or until the little brownies are set; they will have a shiny crust. A toothpick inserted into the center will come out with moist crumbs attached. Don't overbake them or they will be hard.
7. Let the brownie bites cool for 5 minutes, then remove them to a cooling rack. You can eat these warm or cool. Store in an airtight container at room temperature up to 3 days.

Nutrition Info:
- Info Per Serving: Calories: 141 ; Fat: 5 g ;Saturated fat: 2 g ;Sodium: 51 mg

Spicy Tofu Pudding

Servings: 5
Cooking Time: X

Ingredients:

- 1 (3.5 oz) 80% dark chocolate, roughly chopped
- 1 (14 oz) extra-firm tofu, water drained, and tofu patted dry
- 1 tsp vanilla extract
- 1 tsp organic honey
- 1 tsp ground cinnamon
- ¼ tsp cayenne pepper (optional)

Directions:

1. In a medium microwave-safe bowl, heat the chocolate pieces in the microwave for 2 minutes, in 30-second increments until they have melted.
2. In a food processor, add the tofu, vanilla extract, honey, cinnamon, cayenne pepper (if using), and the melted chocolate, blend for 1 minute until smooth, scraping down the sides as needed. Serve as is.

Nutrition Info:

- Info Per Serving: Calories: 131 ; Fat: 18 g ;Saturated fat: 4 g ;Sodium: 11 mg

Apple Pear-nut Crisp

Servings: 8
Cooking Time: X

Ingredients:

- 2 apples, sliced
- 3 pears, sliced
- 2 tablespoons lemon juice
- ¼ cup sugar
- 1 teaspoon cinnamon
- ½ teaspoon nutmeg
- 1½ cups quick-cooking oatmeal
- ½ cup flour
- ¼ cup whole-wheat flour
- ½ cup brown sugar
- 1/3 cup butter or margarine, melted

Directions:

1. Preheat oven to 350°F. Spray a 9″ round cake pan with nonstick cooking spray and set aside.
2. Prepare apples and pears, sprinkling with lemon juice as you work. Combine in medium bowl with sugar, cinnamon, and nutmeg. Spoon into prepared cake pan.
3. In same bowl, combine oatmeal, flour, whole-wheat flour, and brown sugar and mix well. Add melted butter and mix until crumbly. Sprinkle over fruit in dish.
4. Bake for 35–45 minutes or until fruit bubbles and topping is browned and crisp. Let cool for 15 minutes before serving.

Nutrition Info:

- Info Per Serving: Calories: 353.77; Fat:9.97 g ;Saturated fat: 5.25 g;Sodium: 61.78 mg

Appendix A : Measurement Conversions

BASIC KITCHEN CONVERSIONS & EQUIVALENTS

DRY MEASUREMENTS CONVERSION CHART

3 TEASPOONS = 1 TABLESPOON = 1/16 CUP

6 TEASPOONS = 2 TABLESPOONS = 1/8 CUP

12 TEASPOONS = 4 TABLESPOONS = 1/4 CUP

24 TEASPOONS = 8 TABLESPOONS = 1/2 CUP

36 TEASPOONS = 12 TABLESPOONS = 3/4 CUP

48 TEASPOONS = 16 TABLESPOONS = 1 CUP

METRIC TO US COOKING CONVERSIONS

OVEN TEMPERATURES

120 °C = 250 °F

160 °C = 320 °F

180° C = 350 °F

205 °C = 400 °F

220 °C = 425 °F

LIQUID MEASUREMENTS CONVERSION CHART

8 FLUID OUNCES = 1 CUP = 1/2 PINT = 1/4 QUART

16 FLUID OUNCES = 2 CUPS = 1 PINT = 1/2 QUART

32 FLUID OUNCES = 4 CUPS = 2 PINTS = 1 QUART

 = 1/4 GALLON

128 FLUID OUNCES = 16 CUPS = 8 PINTS = 4 QUARTS = 1 GALLON

BAKING IN GRAMS

1 CUP FLOUR = 140 GRAMS

1 CUP SUGAR = 150 GRAMS

1 CUP POWDERED SUGAR = 160 GRAMS

1 CUP HEAVY CREAM = 235 GRAMS

VOLUME

1 MILLILITER = 1/5 TEASPOON

5 ML = 1 TEASPOON

15 ML = 1 TABLESPOON

240 ML = 1 CUP OR 8 FLUID OUNCES

1 LITER = 34 FL. OUNCES

WEIGHT

1 GRAM = .035 OUNCES

100 GRAMS = 3.5 OUNCES

500 GRAMS = 1.1 POUNDS

1 KILOGRAM = 35 OUNCES

US TO METRIC COOKING CONVERSIONS

1/5 TSP = 1 ML

1 TSP = 5 ML

1 TBSP = 15 ML

1 FL OUNCE = 30 ML

1 CUP = 237 ML

1 PINT (2 CUPS) = 473 ML

1 QUART (4 CUPS) = .95 LITER

1 GALLON (16 CUPS) = 3.8 LITERS

1 OZ = 28 GRAMS

1 POUND = 454 GRAMS

BUTTER

1 CUP BUTTER = 2 STICKS = 8 OUNCES = 230 GRAMS = 8 TABLESPOONS

WHAT DOES 1 CUP EQUAL

1 CUP = 8 FLUID OUNCES

1 CUP = 16 TABLESPOONS

1 CUP = 48 TEASPOONS

1 CUP = 1/2 PINT

1 CUP = 1/4 QUART

1 CUP = 1/16 GALLON

1 CUP = 240 ML

BAKING PAN CONVERSIONS

1 CUP ALL-PURPOSE FLOUR = 4.5 OZ

1 CUP ROLLED OATS = 3 OZ 1 LARGE EGG = 1.7 OZ

1 CUP BUTTER = 8 OZ 1 CUP MILK = 8 OZ

1 CUP HEAVY CREAM = 8.4 OZ

1 CUP GRANULATED SUGAR = 7.1 OZ

1 CUP PACKED BROWN SUGAR = 7.75 OZ

1 CUP VEGETABLE OIL = 7.7 OZ

1 CUP UNSIFTED POWDERED SUGAR = 4.4 OZ

BAKING PAN CONVERSIONS

9-INCH ROUND CAKE PAN = 12 CUPS

10-INCH TUBE PAN =16 CUPS

11-INCH BUNDT PAN = 12 CUPS

9-INCH SPRINGFORM PAN = 10 CUPS

9 X 5 INCH LOAF PAN = 8 CUPS

9-INCH SQUARE PAN = 8 CUPS

Appendix B : Recipes Index

Printed in Great Britain
by Amazon